Allison Vale has written more than a dozen books, many of which have indulged a fascination with the obscured lives of women in British history, such as *The Lost Art of Being a Lady, How to Push a Perambulator* and *Amelia Dyer: Angel Maker*, a biography of the murderous, thirty-year career of Britain's most prolific baby farmer. She lives near Bristol with her husband, their two children and an unruly dog named Douglas.

Also by Allison Vale
(co-written with Victoria Ralfs)

How to Raise a Feminist

A Woman Lived Here

....

ALLISON VALE

ROBINSON

ROBINSON

First published in Great Britain in 2018 by
Robinson

This paperback edition published in 2019 by
Robinson

13 5 7 9 10 8 6 4 2

A CIP catalogue record for this book
is available from the British Library.

ISBN: 978-1-47214-356-3

Typeset in Scala by TW Type, Cornwall
Printed and bound in Great Britain by
Clays Ltd, Elcograf S.p.A.

Papers used by Robinson are from well-
managed forests and other responsible sources.

MIX
Paper from
responsible sources
FSC® C104740

Robinson
An imprint of
Little, Brown Book Group
Carmelite House
50 Victoria Embankment
London EC4Y 0DZ

An Hachette UK Company
www.hachette.co.uk

www.littlebrown.co.uk

For Betty and Olwen, remarkable women, always with me

Contents

GREATER LONDON

Region shown in map 2

Region shown in map 3

Region shown in map 4

Region shown in map 5

Acknowledgements

The process of gathering together the fascinating women whose lives contribute to this book has been a team effort.

I am indebted to my sister, Claire, who unearthed a large number of women of science and engineering, as well as musicians and composers for consideration. To Lydia Massiah, for her suggestions of fabulously feisty nineteenth-century feminists. To Tiggi Trethowan, for generously introducing me to the story of her remarkable ancestor, Edith Durham. Thanks to David Walton, without whom I would never have stumbled on the fabulous Beryl Ingham.

To my parents, for their working knowledge of predecimalisation British currency and their skill at adding up, sadly not reliably passed on to their eldest. To Mike, Tom and Louisa for putting up with my endless wittering, and to Vik Ralfs, Alison Rattle, Penny Daly and Maria McCann for their love and encouragement.

Thanks too to my editor, Duncan Proudfoot, for entrusting the book to me; to my agent, Annette Green, for putting her faith in me, and to Amanda Keats and Jane Donovan, whose meticulousness has without doubt made this a far better book.

Introduction

It's possible to walk through the streets of London and glimpse the city through the eyes of past generations; all that's needed is that you keep your eyes up. Look up to the rooflines, strip away the shopfronts and you'll see it: nestled among the shimmering glass towers, concrete multi-storeys and other clusters of twentieth-century development nothing much has changed. What cannot be glimpsed, of course, are the myriad lives of those who once made their home on our streets. The generations of Londoners who lived their best life, each playing their part in making the city what it is today.

The heart and soul of modern London owes a debt of gratitude to the efforts, achievements, sacrifices and selflessness of Londoners past. Some, like George Eliot, the Pankhurst sisters, Sylvia, Christabel and Adela, Florence Nightingale, Mary Shelley and Virginia Woolf, achieved fame and recognition within their own lifetimes and remain household names today. Where the buildings in which these latter-day heroines lived, loved, worked and died stand largely unaltered today, some of these women and their homes have been commemorated by the English Heritage Blue Plaque scheme. At the last count, the scheme honours 903 Londoners, and a walking tour of these sites brings to life the London of a bygone era.

At the time of writing this book, only 111 of these 903 plaques commemorate women. The charity are keenly aware that this imbalance feeds into a common misconception that history has been more impactfully made by men (a recent English Heritage survey found that 40 per cent of us believe men have made a greater contribution to history than women). We're wrong to think this, of course. Women have challenged, changed, built and improved every aspect of life in the capital through the ages. But the source of the misconception is easy to understand: women were largely written out of our history books until the later decades of the twentieth century. Perhaps part of the reason lies in the ebb and flow and diversity of the lives women led; the circuitous paths they were often forced to take in order to achieve success or bring about change. Often, women excelled throughout their lives across a wide array of fields and so left a different kind of paper trail, one which was messier for early modern historians to document than the typically linear career paths of many prominent men.

Aside from the current gender imbalance in the Blue Plaque scheme, there are many more remarkable Londoners who will never be commemorated, simply because the buildings in which they lived or worked no longer survive in any recognisable form. English Heritage stipulate that to qualify for a Blue Plaque, nominees must have lived in London for some significant period of their life (significant in terms of time or accomplishment), have been dead for at least twenty years, and have lived in a house still visible from a public highway in a form that would be largely recognisable to the nominee. In an expanding metropolis, many homes are lost along the way, but it bears saying that this criteria hits hardest those women of London's working classes. Successive generations of the city's working classes lived in slums and poor-quality housing, razed by the Great Fire of London in 1666, in the Edwardian era, in the inter-war and post-war years, or else by the Luftwaffe during the Blitz. Our vision of how London arrived at its current rich, vibrant and diverse state is skewed not only by gender, but also by class: too often, the contributions made by individual working-class Londoners leave too scant a trail for the historian to grapple with.

London's remarkable women deserve to have their stories told, regardless of whether the house they lived in stands today. This book goes a small way towards addressing that loss, commemorating fifty-six women who, at the time of writing, have not been commemorated by the Blue Plaque scheme. Women who set out to make their world a little richer, and in so doing, left an indelible mark on ours. Women who went about their lives quietly but with courage, conviction, skill and compassion, largely unnoticed, even during their own lifetimes. Others who were fearless, strident trailblazers. One or two who used unabashed eccentricity to hold a mirror to the gender restrictions of the day. Many lived in an era when their achievements were given a male name, helping to shroud the capabilities of women outside the home or field. A large proportion of the remarkable women whose lives are recorded on these pages were able to succeed in the way in which they did by forgoing marriage: until 1946, women's contracts were terminated as soon as they married in a vast swathe of areas, including education, retail and the Civil Service.

The women on these pages weren't alone in leaving a remarkable legacy; they weren't always exceptional but they have been singled out here so that their collective stories might build a richer picture of London's past.

Their stories span four hundred years of the capital's history, and the women chronicled on these pages stand testament to the critical role played by London's long and diverse immigrant population, to its visitors and its migrant populations. Women of enormous courage, conviction, faith and creativity, who landed on London soil from every corner of the Earth; women of every race, creed and culture; women who lived out their best lives here, proving themselves to be a vital cog in the capital's story. What emerges too is a sense of a far more complex path to emancipation and equality than simply the suffrage movement or the munitions factory women of the First World War, as vital as they were. In fact, the women of London had been fighting for equality within marriage, the workplace, the law and government for centuries prior to 1919. Progress, when it came, had been the work of generations of brilliant, fearless minds, of every social class, every religion, every race.

This book pays tribute to them all.

Legend:
- – - – Borough boundary
- ● Extant building
- ○ Site of non-extant building

CITY OF LONDON
1 Mary Frith (c. 1584–1659), 133 Fleet Street, Holborn EC4A 2BB.

2 Phillis Wheatley (c. 1753–84), Old Stone Pump, 65–68 Fenchurch Street, Aldgate EC3A 2AD.

3 Rosa Luxemburg (1871–1919), 11 Aldgate High Street, Aldgate EC3N 1AB.

SOUTHWARK
4 Una Marson (1905–65), 164 Queen's Road, Peckham SE15 2DN.

5 Harriet Taylor Mill (1807–58), 277–279 Walworth Road, Walworth SE17 2TG.

6 Elsie Widdowson (1906–2000), 10 Melford Road, Dulwich, SE22 0AD.

LAMBETH
7 Joan Littlewood (1914–2002), 8 Stockwell Road, Brixton SW9.

8 Joan Clarke (1917–96), 45 Idmiston Road, West Norwood SE27 9HL.

LEWISHAM
9 Helen Blackburn (1842–1903), 6 Royal Parade, Blackheath, SE3 0TL.

4

CHAPTER ONE

City of London

ON THE SITE OF 133 FLEET STREET, HOLBORN

In the years before the Great Fire of 1666, Fleet Street was a bustling place, crammed with taverns, meeting houses, butchers, grocers, booksellers, watchmakers, private lodgings and a theatre. Much of the eastern section of Fleet Street, from Fetter Lane east towards Ludgate Hill, would be destroyed by the Great Fire, but in the 1650s, the area reflected a new social diversity, with the emergence of an entrepreneurial middle class for the first time, a product of the social and economic changes which had London in its throes. Fleet Street at this point in history, then, was home to a broad spectrum of London life.

At the eastern end of the street, near its intersections with Shoe Lane and Salisbury Court, stood a popular tavern, the Globe. A few doors down stood the Salisbury Court Theatre, frequented by Samuel Pepys. The Great Conduit was also on this spot – an ingenious medieval gravity-fed water pump, bringing spring water into the city via a tunnel system fashioned from hollowed-out tree trunks. A row of shops advertised their business with brightly coloured emblematic signs hanging precariously above the shopfronts; more than once, a Fleet Street shop sign crashed to the street below, sometimes bringing part of the house down with it. In fact, so perilous were the signs that eventually, in 1767, they were the subject of a parliamentary ruling forcing shopkeepers to attach their signage flat against the wall.

Overlooking the raucous goings-on below was the ancient parish church of St Bride's, served by the eccentric Reverend Palmer, who was said to have saved money to distribute to the poor of the parish by sleeping in the steeple. Eccentricity, in fact, must have seemed commonplace to residents of seventeenth-century Fleet Street, which played constant host to curiosities, roaming entertainers, freak shows and travelling menageries displaying all manner of exotic beasts. With such a concentrated, often migrant population, it's little wonder that the street was also rife with extortion gangs, pickpockets and criminals.

At Fleet Street's intersection with Shoe Lane, where today stand the offices of Goldman Sachs International, was once a row of timber-framed lodgings, and it was here, into a house two doors down from the Globe Tavern, that one of London's most fearless daughters moved in the 1640s.

MARY FRITH
(c. 1584–1659)

Sometimes it takes a truly irrepressible, untameable spirit to confront the most deeply embedded of society's gender restrictions. A woman not afraid to risk notoriety, not shy of criminality, if that's what it takes to live her best life – a 'Roaring Girl'. In seventeenth-century London, Mary Frith proved herself eminently up to that task.

Born into what appears to have been a respectable enough, hard-working family, Mary was said to have raged against convention from childhood. In her youth, her family staged something of an intervention, her cleric uncle arranging for her to be carried off to a ship docked at Gravesend and sent to New England for a fresh start. The story goes that Frith couldn't be contained, jumping ship in the harbour and swimming ashore. From this distance, it's impossible to sift through the myth to find the truth; there were many stories. Certainly at the age of sixteen, Frith had already been arrested for theft, though that was a common enough phenomenon in every era of London's history. What made this arrest all the more significant was that this was also the earliest recorded occasion on which she was said to have caused consternation by appearing in public dressed in a man's doublet and breeches, with a smoking pipe in her hand.

In 1600, cross-dressing was restricted to life onstage. Elizabethan theatre was an exclusively male domain, a profession regarded as too unseemly for a woman. Later in the century, after the cultural dearth of Puritanism gave way to the Restoration, women did enter the theatre via the stage door, and began to enjoy considerable fame as a consequence. But in 1600, male to female cross-dressing was a standard source of entertainment. Female to male cross-dressing was an entirely more controversial phenomenon, for which women were whipped and pilloried and demonised as loose-moralled harlots.

This was an era of state-enforced dress codes, with fabrics such as silk, colours such as purple and accessories such as gold restricted by law to a privileged core within society. Clothing in 1600 was a uniform, strictly overseen as a means of maintaining an explicit and self-evident social order, within which women were subordinate. To cross-dress was to subvert that order and was therefore regarded with suspicion and condemnation. In Elizabethan London for the first time, it became increasingly difficult to judge a person's class on their appearance alone: entrepreneurialism had given rise to social climbing on an unprecedented scale, enabling Londoners to access luxuries that had been beyond the reach of the class into which they were born. Efforts to control costume and clothing were in some respects a knee-jerk reaction to these changes; straying from the norm by dressing outside your gender or class happened, but was especially denounced. Women who stepped outside of convention by donning male clothing were seen to be dangerously lacking in self-control and moral fortitude; cross-dressing was therefore highly salacious, widely regarded as synonymous with prostitution, making it even more exposing for Frith to have cross-dressed in public.

Mary Frith was having none of it. Defiant in the face of all efforts to contain her, she embraced criminality, supporting herself by working the streets in the way male criminals were doing all around her. At least four times, she was apprehended and punished by having the palms of her hands burned; it did nothing to curb her habits. The broadsheets loved her and loathed her in equal measure and her unconventional spirit brought her to wide public attention: within ten years of her first arrest, she had already been the subject of three stage plays, and was widely referred to as 'Moll Cutpurse', a reference both to her perceived licentious sexuality ('Molls' were prostitutes) and her crimes (street thieves typically slashed the cord which attached a coin purse to the waist).

In 1611, Frith took her defiance a step further, appearing onstage at the Fortune Playhouse, a wooden, open-roofed theatre just outside the City walls, that was a contemporary to both the Globe Theatre and the Swan Theatre. She entertained her audience with bawdy songs, accompanied herself on the lute and dressed as she always did, in knee breeches and jerkin, scandalously puffing on a pipe (smoking, for women, was also outlawed). She made an impromptu appearance too onstage at the Fortune, in a production called *Amends for Ladies*. The play told its own version of the life of Moll Cutpurse. It capitalised on Frith's notoriety, wanting to throw into stark relief the undesirability of her unconventional lifestyle by having her appear alongside demure, restrained female characters. Historians suspect that neither the playwright nor the players intended that the real Moll Cutpurse should actually appear before the audience, but appear she did, challenging their speculation as to her gender and in doing so entirely undermining the impact of the (male) actor playing her part. If the play was intended to take the spotlight of celebrity away from Frith, it failed, only serving to heighten public interest in her across the city.

On Christmas Day that same year, the authorities finally caught up with Frith, arresting her for appearing in public as a man, an offence they deemed 'lewd behaviour'. They cited as supporting evidence her habit of frequenting 'alehowses Tavernes Tobacco shops' while dressed as a man; they implied an involvement in prostitution, though failed to cite any specific instance, her immorality in other respects deemed evidence enough. Her specific crime was her appearance on stage at the Fortune Theatre – outlawed for women at the time. Her punishment was to make public penance, draped in white, at an open-air preaching ground in London called St Paul's Cross; the crowd took her incoherent wailing as a sign of penitence when in fact she was incoherently drunk. The experience was of no consequence for Frith, who by now, knew how to work an audience, and she would later boast she would happily have played every market in England.

Frith's life continued to play out with much drama, from her incarceration in the notorious London asylum for the insane, Bethlem, to Civil War days as a pro-Royalist highwaywoman, and her subsequent narrow escape from the gallows of Newgate. All were chronicled in *The Life of Mrs Mary Frith*, an autobiography penned by Frith in the last years of her life, though laden with exaggeration. It was published in 1662, three years after her death from dropsy, the first autobiography of a female criminal ever published in England, sealing her notoriety for centuries to come.

Frith's criminality had been only a part of her story. Conventional marriage or a life of quiet service, lived largely indoors and out of sight, had been unthinkable, as too, were the strict dress codes of Elizabethan society. With enormous courage and an unstoppably rebellious spirit, Mary Frith stepped outside of all expectations and in so doing challenged those around her to reconsider the perceived wisdom which saw women as incapable of steering their own course without descending into promiscuity. Like the 'roaring boys' who picked fights on London's streets, she roared at the pervasive patriarchy of seventeenth-century London and for that is worthy of commemoration.

87 FENCHURCH STREET (NOW RAZED), ON THE SITE OF 65–68 FENCHURCH STREET, NEAR THE OLD STONE PUMP, FENCHURCH STREET, ALDGATE

In 1761, the gate which had stood at the easternmost section of London's city wall since Roman times was finally demolished. Named Aldgate, it had been rebuilt and renovated several times over the centuries, to include, for instance, the addition of an upper-floor apartment in the gatehouse, briefly the damp, dark and uncomfortable home of medieval poet, Geoffrey Chaucer. Today, nothing much survives of eighteenth-century Aldgate, aside from the name and four places of worship: the parish churches of St Katherine Cree, near Leadenhall Market, St Botolph's, at Aldgate High Street, St Andrew Undershaft, which survived both the Great Fire and the Blitz, and the Bevis Marks Synagogue, dating back to 1699.

At the junction of Aldgate and Fenchurch Street, however, there remains a Victorian replica of a key local landmark dating back centuries: the old stone pump. The pump was the point from which distances to Norwich and other locations to the east of London were measured and it came to symbolise the start of London's East End. The Victorians converted the pump into a public drinking fountain in the 1870s, drawing from an underground stream. In a macabre gothic twist, it was soon discovered that the water's peculiar taste was due to calcium contamination from corpses buried in the many cemeteries through which the stream ran.

In the autumn of 1773, the original pump would have been a key landmark for which Nathaniel Wheatley, a visitor to the city that season, would certainly have been on the lookout. Wheatley, the son of a wealthy Boston, New England, merchant, was making his first visit to the Aldgate offices of bookseller Archibald Bell, himself a Bostonian. In Bell's trade directory advertisements he also promised, 'Printing In all its Branches neatly Executed' and helped prospective customers locate his premises at 87 Fenchurch Street, with the direction, 'Near the Stone Pump, Aldgate'. It was Bell's printing press that was of interest to Wheatley that day, though he himself was not a writer; his business with Bell was on behalf of a frail and deferential 19-year-old West African woman walking a few steps behind him, into Bell's Aldgate offices.

PHILLIS WHEATLEY
(c. 1753–84)

Phillis Wheatley had been captured from her home in West Africa at the age of around seven, and forced onto a slave ship, the *Phillis*, bound for North America. Robbed of her homeland, her family and her childhood, by the time she reached the port in Boston she had been deprived, too, of her birth-name. She arrived along with a cargo of West Africans who had, like her, been deemed too frail to endure the labours of the West Indian plantations and so had been brought on to Boston. At the port, she was bought by a wealthy merchant named John Wheatley to work as a domestic servant for his wife, Susanna; Wheatley had been able to secure himself a bargain that day, purchasing the child 'for a trifle' because the ship's captain, who suspected the child was close to death, had been keen to get her off his hands. The Wheatley family later recalled that the girl they had named after the slave ship arrived emaciated and almost entirely naked, wrapped in a piece of filthy carpet.

Very quickly, the family learned something else about the child in their charge: she was fiercely intelligent. Within a very short space of time, she gained a fluency in English and under the tutelage of the Wheatleys' 18-year-old twins, Mary and Nathaniel, read voraciously. Astronomy, history, geography, the Bible, the works of John Milton and Alexander Pope, along with the classics – Ovid, Homer, Virgil. She began to write poetry, reflecting the broad array of subjects in which she took an interest, and within a decade, had a collection of twenty-eight poems of significant lyricism and delicacy.

For an enslaved person to have been enabled to become literate was rare enough in eighteenth-century North America; an enslaved poet was something else entirely. The Wheatleys saw an opportunity and embarked upon a marketing campaign, publishing her poems in newspapers and periodicals in an effort to get her name known and secure enough subscribers to support publication. The poetry drew heavily from the Christian context of Phillis Wheatley's education: her early poem, 'On Being Brought from Africa to America', appears to sing out in praise of the traffic in human life which 'brought me from my Pagan land', for instance.

Boston's elite weren't convinced: many were proponents of the insidious view that black Africans were inherently uneducable. Against that context, few were prepared to accept the child had authored the poems herself. To combat this, in the autumn of 1872, John Wheatley had gathered together in Boston's Old Town Hall eighteen of the town's leading politicians and thinkers. All were men; most were Harvard graduates and the majority were slave owners. Into this company, 18-year-old Phillis was led. The men grilled her, struggling to find a means with which they could uncover what they had been convinced was a sham. At length, they failed in their mission and reluctantly declared her a prodigy, signing an affidavit testifying that they, 'some of the best Judges', considered her 'qualified to write'. John Wheatley hoped this would generate enough interest to secure an audience for publication in New England. It didn't. Hungry for fame, the family turned their attention to London, where one of Phillis's poems had received the support of the influential Countess of Huntingdon and had subsequently been published in London in 1771. This gave Phillis Wheatley a sizeable English fan base, prompting the family to approach the Countess asking for an introduction to an English publisher.

So it was that Nathaniel and Phillis found themselves on Fenchurch Street, as part of a six-week visit to the capital in 1773. Phillis's correspondence from the time reveals that she was giddied by the attention she received in London. Her name and reputation had gone before her and she was greeted as something of a celebrity, entertained by some impressive society including the Lord Mayor of London, the Earl of Dartmouth and even George Washington. Significantly, she also spent time in the company of leading abolitionist, Granville Sharp, who took her on a tour of the Tower of London and London Zoo.

The meeting marked a turning point in Wheatley's life, with implications far beyond her literary career. This was largely because of the historical context of her visit. A year before her arrival, London had been rocked by a legal battle presided over by Lord Mansfield, Lord Chief Justice on the King's Bench. Mansfield had ruled that slave owners could not compel their slaves to return to the colonies once on English soil, effectively rendering them free for as long as they remained in the country. The case had a huge impact on both sides of the Atlantic and had been highly publicised in New England, not least in several of the newspapers in which Wheatley's poems regularly featured. It seems highly likely that Wheatley would have been fully aware that her presence in London would not only help launch her career as a poet, but could also secure her freedom.

The subject must have been discussed on the day Wheatley and Sharp toured the captive animals of Africa trapped behind bars at the

London Zoo; it seems highly unlikely that Sharp, in the company of an enslaved young woman, would have passed up the opportunity to encourage her to seek freedom. Their conversations are not recorded in any detail in Phillis Wheatley's diaries. In any case, after a whirlwind six weeks, Phillis, though not Nathaniel, cut short her stay to make the return crossing to North America, ostensibly following news that her mistress, Susanna Wheatley, had been taken ill and was in need of her care. An Atlantic crossing took on average five weeks in 1773: word of an illness in Boston could hardly have reached London in so short a time, prompting some to speculate that Wheatley, perhaps steered by Granville, may have carefully negotiated the terms of her return with her owner, via Nathaniel, before stepping off English soil. Certainly, upon her return to the Wheatley household, she was manumitted and in a letter sent soon after, she referred to her freedom as having resulted from 'the desire of my friends in England'.

London had secured Phillis's freedom, but it had also been successful in its other aim. John Wheatley had ensured that a steady stream of new poems had been fed to the British press both ahead of and during Phillis's stay. In New England he had worked equally hard to keep interest high in 'the extraordinary Negro poet', publishing a succession of her poems, as well as news pieces about Phillis's progress on her foreign trip. Affirming Phillis's celebrity in London and capitalising on the high status of her British patrons enabled the big push they had hoped for and they were finally able to secure her a publication deal in New England.

Her book, *Poems on Subjects Religious and Moral*, was published to some fanfare in London by Archibald Bell from his Fenchurch Street press in 1773. In a pre-publication advertisement in the British press, Bell ensured there was no question of the inherent genius of its author, informing any who didn't already know that Wheatley had been 'born in the wilds of Africa', though carefully omitting her enslaved status. Inside the front cover, Bell had gone to the extraordinary lengths of including an engraving of the author; this rare frontispiece was done at the suggestion of the Countess of Huntingdon and would have added to Wheatley's celebrity in England. To Bostonians, it would have seemed quite astonishing: for an enslaved person to have had their portrait done in any circumstance was almost unheard of, and those few known to have been undertaken were of men. Wheatley was the first woman of African descent to have sat for her own portrait; the depiction of her sat reading and writing, pen in hand, was revolutionary given the context of colonial slavery and the widely held fallacy that Africans were intellectually inferior.

The book was the first ever authored by a black African-American woman and its impact was of enormous significance. Abolitionists often cited Wheatley's work as evidence of the inherent equality of the races. To assuage the many sceptics, the signed testimony of the eighteen Bostonian dignitaries was also included in the book; in the eighteenth century, it wasn't enough that an African woman could write beautiful, contemplative poetry. She had also to prove to a predominantly white, male audience that she had written it.

Freedom marked a change in the tone of Wheatley's writing. She began to assert her own part in her literary success, where previously she had simply expressed a demure gratitude for the critical role others had had on her behalf. Critically, buoyed by her release, she began to take an overt anti-slavery stance in her work for the first time. Manumission, however, brought with it new hardships. Wheatley experienced first-hand the poverty typically endured by free African-Americans in the era: such was the extent of deprivation that to those living it, it must have felt like enslavement in a new guise. Wheatley's life took on a level of hardship that was entirely new to her. She married, had two children, both of whom died in infancy, and saw her husband imprisoned for debt. Her pre-Revolutionary war patrons had long since abandoned her and she tried and failed to secure the publication of a second volume of her poetry. She continued to publish occasionally in newspapers but took work as a scullery maid in order to survive, living out her last days in desperate circumstances. She died in 1784 at the age of thirty-one, weeks after the death of her last child.

For a few brief but critical years in the 1770s, Phillis Wheatley had been hailed as 'the most famous African on the face of the earth', praised by the likes of Voltaire and George Washington. She was a true pioneer, shattering some of the most sinister doctrines underpinning the continuing traffic in human life, and her work marked the start of a growing canon of African-American writers. Her visit to Archibald Bell, alongside Aldgate's old stone pump in 1773, had marked a crucial turning point in her life, enabling her transition from hobby-poet to professional writer; from slave to freewoman.

11 ALDGATE HIGH STREET, THE SITE OF THE THREE NUNS HOTEL (RAZED IN THE 1960S), ALDGATE

ROSA LUXEMBURG
(1871–1919)

Rosa Luxemburg was born into a Jewish family in Poland and spent her early adulthood as a journalist. She was a passionate believer in socialist political principles and an outspoken critic of the First World War, regarding it as a capitalist exercise in pitting workers against each other, views for which she was imprisoned for much of the war. She developed Communist principles and established the German Communist Party in 1918 and co-founded the revolutionary group, the Spartacist League, with German socialist Karl Liebknecht in 1914. Throughout her life she lived in Europe, but made the journey to London in May 1907 to attend the Russian Social Democrats' Fifth Party Day – a visit that would prove a significant turning point in her political career. It was in London in 1907 that Luxemburg first met Vladimir Lenin. She recorded her unease with her choice of venue for her stay in London: she had booked into London's oldest tavern, the Three Nuns in Whitechapel, said to have dated back to the time of Daniel Defoe. Her private correspondence revealed the extent of her distaste for the Three Nuns: '*Why, the very name is suspicious as hell*'.

CHAPTER TWO

Southwark

---

164 QUEEN'S ROAD, PECKHAM

At 164 Queen's Road, Peckham, almost at its junction with St Mary's Road, is a whitewashed Georgian home, indicative of Peckham's early nineteenth-century roots, when much of the area was rural or given over to market gardening. There is already a Blue Plaque on the house, commemorating a Jamaican doctor named Harold Moody, who came to London in 1904 to study medicine and opened his own practice in 1913. Moody experienced first-hand the significant barrier his racial origin presented in London and so founded the League of Coloured Peoples in 1931 and made sure his doors were always open to 'all travelling black people who couldn't find a room or a meal elsewhere'. And so, in 1932, he welcomed a new Jamaican visitor to the city, a single woman who would use her gift for the written word to throw a spotlight of her own on the racism and inequality inherent in London life.

UNA MARSON

(1905–65)

When Una Marson first arrived in London in 1932 from her native Jamaica, she was already a journalist, a poet with two published collections behind her, and a critically acclaimed playwright. In 1928, she had been the first Jamaican woman ever to have launched her own magazine. Still only twenty-seven years old, she had dedicated her work to encouraging Jamaican women to politicise themselves, to join the work force and to make their voices heard. But at this stage Marson was very much a product of the Empire, her work grounded in English literary traditions. London was to change all that.

In the capital, she encountered racism on such a prolific scale that it seeped through the pores of everything she wrote. She drew upon the success of her first play, *At What Price*, to fund a London staging, which opened within the year, making Marson's the first all-black production ever staged in the city. A year after her arrival, she wrote a powerful poem tackling the issue of racism in London for Moody's *League of Coloured Peoples'* journal, *The Keys*. Called 'Nigger', the poem describes an encounter on a London street with a group of children, 'little white urchins', who hurl racial abuse at her as she passes. It traces the roots of the word back to slavery and criticises those who purport to be Christian and yet think nothing of using the word to insult the city's black population. It marked a turning point in her work.

Marson began to use her literary prowess to highlight feminist and racist issues confronting London's Jamaican population on a daily basis. She tackled, too, the insidious pull of the ideals of female beauty as portrayed in the movie industry and worked hard to call for Jamaican women to celebrate beauty that was not white-skinned or straight-haired. She joined the International Alliance of Women for Equal Suffrage and Citizenship and was the only black delegate at the Alliance's conference in Istanbul in 1935. Her attention shifted to tackle the colour bar she had encountered first-hand when first seeking employment in London.

After a two-year return to Jamaica, in 1938 she was back in London. Her drive now was to celebrate Jamaican culture in her poetry and plays: she established her own Jamaican-based publishing press, The Pioneer Press, and did much to advance, promote and celebrate the country's rich literary and cultural traditions. Her involvement in international politics led to her appointment as the private secretary of Haile Selassie, the Emperor of Ethiopia, in which role she did much to highlight the atrocities inflicted on the women of Ethiopia during Italian occupation.

Her poetry was as lyrical and beguiling as it was strident and hard-hitting. In 1938, she staged her third play, *Pocomania*, which examined the impact of indigenous Jamaican religion on a dissatisfied and restless middle-class Jamaican woman. The play was delivered in the Jamaican language, throughout which Marson wove traditional proverbs, songs and dance. *Pocomania* helped push to the fore an inherently Jamaican literary and cultural tradition, as a counter-movement to the restrictive voice of the Empire which had first shaped her as a woman and a writer.

In 1941, Marson achieved another important first for women of colour living in the UK when she became the first black woman to be employed at the BBC, working initially as programme assistant with the Empire Service and quickly being called upon by George Orwell to contribute to his literary radio programme, *Voices*. In 1942, she made history again, becoming the first black woman broadcaster, launching her own radio programme, *Caribbean Voices*. Its significance extended beyond the fact of her voice at the helm: Caribbean voices read Caribbean poetry out over the airwaves, helping to establish the genre as a predominantly spoken medium.

Marson is commemorated for her commitment to celebrating an indigenous Jamaican literary tradition; for her belief in the power of the written word to foster a robust cultural identity and pride; for her dedication to global feminism, and for the fearless way in which she used her own experience to raise the profile of the very real issues facing the Caribbean diaspora in London. And it was at the home of Dr Harold Moody, with its warm welcome and wide open doors, where she first channelled her experience of the racism running through the heart of London culture into powerful verse, marking a shift in her focus that would be of enormous cultural, literary and political importance.

277–279 *WALWORTH ROAD, FORMERLY 8 BECKFORD ROW, WALWORTH*

HARRIET TAYLOR MILL
(1807–58)
At the age of twenty-four, Harriet Taylor, the wife of a Walworth druggist, was already a published essayist with a growing reputation for her brilliant mind and for her feminist treaties on employment,

equality of opportunity and domestic violence. Her life was to take an unexpected turn when she met the philosopher John Stuart Mill at a dinner party. The two embarked upon an extended love affair, which led to the amicable but unconventional end of her marriage to Taylor. Harriet and John eventually married on Taylor's death. Harriet's words and philosophies were embedded, though unacknowledged, within the heart of the most enduring works published by her second husband, her views more radical than his own in many respects. Mill held his wife's intellect in higher regard than his own and later in life credited Harriet as having co-authored many of his most significant works and as having edited them all, though she was never officially named as co-author in print.

Harriet had been born at 8 Beckford Row, a generous Georgian home which was converted into a retail outlet by the Victorians, the shopfront extending into what was once a small front garden.

10 MELFORD ROAD, DULWICH, SOUTHWARK

ELSIE WIDDOWSON
(1906–2000)

Elsie Widdowson had one of the most remarkable scientific careers of the twentieth century. One of Imperial College, London's first female graduates, she went on to gain a PhD and a doctorate in biochemistry. She specialised in dietetics and nutrition, work which was of critical importance during the Second World War, when her findings about the health impact of a restricted diet and nutritional supplements were to become central to the Ministry of Food's rationing programmes. Later, she was consulted for the nutritional support, treatment and rehabilitation of the survivors of concentration camps. Her post-war work on infant nutrition led to improvements in formula baby milk.

Widdowson was raised in the small Georgian terrace at 10 Melford Road, Dulwich.

CHAPTER THREE

Lambeth

....

8 STOCKWELL ROAD (NOW RAZED), BRIXTON

By the 1920s, Stockwell Road and the surrounding area of Brixton was South London's most thriving shopping centre, boasting Britain's first purpose-built department store, the Bon Marché, which opened in 1877. The beautiful Astoria Cinema, with its plush interior and proscenium arch, opened on Stockwell Road in 1929 and survives to this day, renamed the Brixton Academy.

Surrounded by largely working-class housing, it was an area rich in culture. Its early origins were rooted in privilege: four of an original nine pairs of grey-stone terraces survive at numbers 40 to 46, echoing the grander days of late eighteenth-century Stockwell. By the turn of the twentieth century, however, it was home to a large population of hard-working, working-class families, housed in Victorian terraces that were razed in the decades after the Second World War to make way for large blocks of flats. Number 8, Stockwell Road was among those houses lost. The census of 1911 lists number 8 as a home of seven rooms, occupied by telegraph linesman Robert Littlewood, his wife, Caroline Emily, their four children, ranging in age from twenty-two to sixteen years, and three boarders taken in to help make ends meet. Every member of the household worked: the youngest, Kate, aged just sixteen in 1911, was a brush finisher – sanding, staining and polishing handmade brushes. Three years later, at the age of nineteen and still unmarried, Kate gave birth to a daughter who would change the face of British theatre.

JOAN LITTLEWOOD
(1914–2002)

Once in every era comes a woman so strident in her beliefs, so bent on bringing into being what she perceives to be lacking in her world, that she changes everything. A one-woman revolution no less. Joan Littlewood was that woman.

Joan was born into poverty, to a teenage single mother who had been earning her living in the brush-making industry in working-class Stockwell. She had a stormy relationship with her mother, ran away frequently and was raised mostly by her grandparents. Many, including Joan herself, report she harboured a sense of angry injustice from an early age, berating her grandfather at the age of twelve, for instance, when the General Strike of 1926 came to a halt after just ten days. Her fierce intellect and inquisitive mind was at odds within a largely illiterate family and she recalls sloping off in secret to the library whenever she could, to read the books her mother would threaten to throw on the fire, if caught.

Joan became fascinated with the stage, watching as many productions as she could in her teens and standing judgement over Gielgud's *Macbeth* at the Old Vic, determining to stage her own production at school to right his mistakes. Later, she won the only London scholarship to RADA, where her rage at the clipped, patrician accents of finishing-school privilege drove her to set off for the US, beginning the journey by heading to Liverpool on foot. (She made it as far as Burton-on-Trent, where she collapsed and was given the bus fare to Manchester by a kindly stranger.)

In Manchester she felt more at ease and she stayed there throughout the 1930s and into the war years. She discovered agitprop theatre, thanks to folk singer Ewan MacColl, her first husband, and together they set up Theatre Union, drawing wide influence from Soviet theatre, Brecht, Stanislavski and Laban, before British theatre was even really aware of them. She increasingly bedded everything she did in her passion for *commedia dell'arte*, the sixteenth-century radical theatre of the people. By 1945, with her marriage to MacColl over and Theatre Union having been joined by public-school runaway and teen communist, Gerry Raffles, she renamed the company 'Theatre Workshop', drew up a manifesto, hired a van and went on tour for eight years, including taking in Russia, where she said she finally found people who took theatre seriously. At last, in February 1953, Theatre Workshop found themselves in a rundown variety theatre in the East End of London, which they made their home.

Theatre Workshop was like nothing British theatre had ever seen before. They were a permanent troupe, with their own in-house writers, actors and directors. The old Theatre Royal at Stratford East became a squat, with gas burners and sleeping bags and water buckets to catch the deluge pouring from a leaking roof. Together, they produced some of the finest plays of the mid-twentieth century, including *Oh! What a Lovely War*, Shelagh Delaney's *A Taste of Honey* and Brendan Behan's *The Quare Fellow*. She gave local East End talent such as Michael Caine and Barbara Windsor a start and the company's reputation grew.

Littlewood's rage, however, never abated. She had dreamt of creating a working-class revolution in theatre – finding and nurturing working-class talent so as to stage productions for the working classes, *by* the working classes. She wanted to shatter the fourth wall between cast and audience once and for all, making theatre a truly communal experience and, to that end, had Victor Spinetti come out on stage between scenes in the peerless *Oh! What a Lovely War* to talk to the audience – *really* talk. Unscripted.

But her dream would ultimately become a victim of its own success: production after production transferred to the West End and while the income from transfers enabled Theatre Workshop's survival, as well as steadily wearing away at the staid convention of much of pre-war drama, it brought with it popularity. The audiences who flocked to Stratford East by the late fifties were not the working classes of the East End, but the wealthy, fur-clad middle class of West London. And the West End transfers began to dwindle Littlewood's company, as more and more of the talent she nurtured were swept on to glittering careers in commercial theatre.

The final triumph for the company – the moment they were able to buy the theatre – was the moment Littlewood chose to step away. Commercial success had been very far from her goal: the radical way in which she rehearsed and staged *Oh! What a Lovely War* was unlike anything the British stage had seen and she warned her cast not to expect critics to like it. She had revolutionised the way writers wrote for theatre, the way directors staged their productions and the way companies rehearsed and grew. After the mid-seventies she produced very little, but by that time London boasted more than a hundred fringe theatre groups, none of which had existed before. Joan Littlewood had fundamentally changed British theatre with her vision of a new era of community theatre that was altogether more gritty, more organic and more radical, and however dissatisfied she may have felt with the end result, her vision has nonetheless been kept alive.

45 IDMISTON ROAD, WEST NORWOOD

Number 45, Idmiston Road is a generous, double-fronted Victorian villa a short stroll from the site of a former Anglican parish church. The church was felled by a direct hit from a German V2 bomb in 1944, along with several of the surrounding houses. Number 45 escaped intact, and stands to this day. It was here that the Reverend William Clarke moved prior to the First World War from Suffolk, to take up a new position at the local parish church. His youngest child, Joan, was born at number 45 in 1917. Joan was to prove herself one of the nation's finest minds.

JOAN CLARKE
(1917–96)

In an era when women's intellectual capabilities were still poorly regarded, Joan Clarke's life and work is significant: not only did she prove she was more than a match for her male peers, but she used the weight of her intellect to help change the course of the Second World War.

Clarke was lauded by all who knew and worked with her as an unassuming, diffident young woman, a gifted mathematician who nonetheless deferred to the men in her life in all things, as was typical of so many women of the era. She was educated at Cambridge, where she achieved a double First in her Tripos in Mathematics in

1939, and where her mathematical prowess was noted by her geometry supervisor, Gordon Welchman. With the outbreak of the Second World War in that same year, Welchman was approached by the British government to establish a cryptography operation at Bletchley Park in Buckinghamshire, one of only four mathematicians to have been recruited to work to decode German radio communications. Welchman gathered a team and asked Clarke to join him while she was in her final year at Cambridge. She was the only woman recruited to the role of cryptanalyst, a task so sensitive that initially, she was given no detail beyond a vague mention that it would actually require no mathematics, 'but mathematicians tended to be good at it'. Despite the intrigue (or perhaps, in part, because of it), Clarke agreed, and joined the team in June 1939.

She found herself the only woman in an all-male world; the only other women at Bletchley Park were either secretarial staff or translators. Clarke joined a team challenged with decoding Enigma, the complex German encryption device, although she was paid significantly less than her male counterparts to do so. She excelled and was quickly given her own desk in a small team in Hut 8, working with Alan Turing on German Naval Enigma, said to have been the toughest of the different types of Enigma encryption to crack.

By 1941, Turing had devised a complex method of decoding the Naval Enigma with a device he named the 'Banburismus'. Clarke proved to be the most adept and enthusiastic of all the cryptanalysts working with the Banburismus and the work brought her and Turing close. She later recalled that one day, to her surprise, he suddenly proposed marriage, which she accepted, delightedly. The following day, he told her he doubted the engagement could succeed and admitted his true sexuality. The engagement didn't immediately come to an end, and although it was ultimately called off, Clarke and Turing remained close until his suicide in 1954.

Clarke remained at Hut 8 for the duration of the war, promoted to deputy head of the team in 1944. At the end of the war, Bletchley Park was disbanded and the team dispersed, but she was to continue her work as a codebreaker within the newly formed GCHQ for the rest of her career. She was awarded an MBE in 1947 for services to the war effort, although the restrictions of the Official Secrets Act meant that no details of her war work could be made public. But without a doubt, her dedication as a codebreaker during the war years was pivotal to the Allied victory in Europe.

CHAPTER FOUR

Lewisham

6 ROYAL PARADE, BLACKHEATH

HELEN BLACKBURN
(1842–1903)

Blackburn was an early women's rights campaigner, a key member of the Langham Place Group, for whom she edited *The Englishwoman's Review*. She helped spearhead the Group's campaigns to address gender discrimination in British employment laws and worked tirelessly to raise awareness of the insufferable conditions endured by women factory workers.

Blackburn lived in Blackheath after moving from Ireland in 1859. In her early years, she established a reputation as a talented artist, but her career was curtailed at a young age when her eyesight deteriorated. Despite poor health, she was held in high regard among her contemporaries for her vast body of knowledge and her ceaseless call for equal employment conditions and opportunities for women.

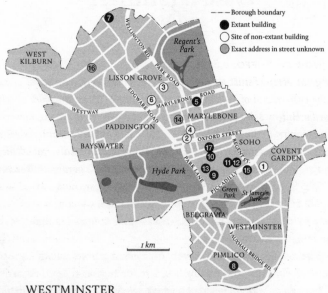

WESTMINSTER

1 **Patience Lovell Wright** (1725–86), 22 Suffolk Street, Strand SW1Y 4HG.

2 **Mary Anning** (1799–1847), 3 Bryanston Street, Marylebone W1H 7BY.

3 **Barbara Leigh Smith Bodichon** (1827–91), 5 Blandford Square, Marylebone W1U 3DB.

4 **Ethel Smyth** (1858–1944), Portman Square, Wigmore Street, Marylebone W1U 8EW.

5 **Louisa Aldrich-Blake** (1865–1925), 17 Nottingham Place, Marylebone W1U 5LG.

6 **Eliza Armstrong** (1872–1938), 32 Ranston Street, Marylebone NW1 6SY.

7 **Caroline Harriet Haslett** (1895–1957), 2 Springfield Road, Marylebone NW8 0QN.

8 **Isadora Duncan** (1877–1927), 33 Warwick Square, Pimlico SW1V 2AQ.

9 **Caroline Norton** (1808–77), Chesterfield Street, Mayfair W1J 5JF.

10 **Lady Evelyn Zainab Cobbold** (1867–1963), 9 Carlos Place, Mayfair W1K 3AT.

11 **Gertrude Jekyll** (1843–1932), 2 Grafton Street, Mayfair W1S 4FE.

12 **Claude Cahun** (1894–1954), Royal Academy of Arts, Burlington Gardens, Mayfair W1S.

13 **Anne McLaren** (1927–2007), Aberconway House, 38 South Street, Mayfair W1K 1DJ.

14 **Lady Hester Stanhope** (1776–1839), Montagu Square, Marylebone, W1H.

15 **Fanny Cornforth** (1835–1909), 96 Jermyn Street, St James's, SW1Y 6JE.

16 **Countess Emilie Lind af Hageby** (1878–1963), and **Leisa Schartau** (1876–1961), Lauderdale Mansions, Maida Vale, W9 1NE.

17 **Edith Durham** (1863–1944), 82 Brook Street, near Hanover Square, Mayfair W1K 5EQ.

CHAPTER FIVE

Westminster

---

30 (NOW 22) SUFFOLK STREET, STRAND

The great sweep of stuccoed properties on Suffolk Street, a quiet cul-de-sac off the eastern end of Pall Mall, were built in the 1820s, the work of cele-brated architect, John Nash. A century before Nash's renovations, however, the area surrounding the street was still predominantly rural. Leicester Square was Leicester Fields, common land on which locals grazed their livestock, with a large portion enclosed as the private gardens of the 2nd Earl of Leicester. Several of the surrounding street names hark back to these pastoral origins, including Haymarket and Hedge Lane, both once very literal descriptions. John Strype in his extensive Survey of London *of 1720, referred to the Haymarket as a particularly busy thoroughfare, especially on Tuesdays, Thursdays and Saturdays when a market selling hay and straw took place.*

Those who were resident in the area by the late seventeenth century were largely privileged: diarist Samuel Pepys specifically mentioned Suffolk Street in connection with an actress named Moll Davis, a courtesan of Charles II. Pepys wrote that in 1672, the King had furnished Davis with her own home, 'in Suffolk Street most richly', equipped with an elaborate coach, about which Pepys fails to disguise his envy. It would have been one of the homes Stype would describe a few decades later as the street's 'handsome Houses'.

By the later decades of the eighteenth century the area was no longer exclusively residential, with places of commerce and leisure springing up on every street, and the homes that had once been the classy choice for a royal courtesan were now at least a century old and could no longer have been quite so handsome. The British Library holds an impeccably drawn pen-and-ink map of Suffolk Street and its environs from this period, prior to Nash's transformation, drawn up by surveyor Thomas Chawner in 1796. On Chawner's plan, a tavern, the Rising Sun, stood on the corner of

Suffolk Street, at the southern face of its junction with Little Suffolk Street. Next-door-but-one to the tavern was number 30, the spot now occupied by number 22. It was to this house, in what was fast emerging as a cultural hub of the city, that an eccentric New England widow and her five children moved in 1772. Though a first-time visitor to London, she would soon make herself known in the most remarkable manner.

PATIENCE LOVELL WRIGHT
(1725–86)

Patience Lovell Wright's arrival in London in 1772 had been something of a leap of faith. A striking woman, tall and, by reputation, loquacious, she left behind her in the colony a well-established business and, crucially, a reputation. In London, she was effectively starting over, pinning her fortunes on the clout of leading New Englander, Benjamin Franklin, who had not yet founded an independent America, and who had believed in her sufficiently to promise introductions to the very best of London society.

Wright had already lived an extraordinary life, even by the standards of the day. Born to a wealthy Quaker farmer on Long Island, her childhood had been sanitised and bleached by her father's idiosyncrasies. His imposition of a vegetarian regimen, unusual enough in its day, was one Patience found entirely tolerable ('that is the reason we are all so ingenious,' she would later remark). Far less so was his other stipulation: no colour. John Lovell forbade his family to wear anything but white. Unsurprisingly, in the circumstances, Patience and her sister, Rachel, turned to art to lend vibrancy to what became an increasingly dispiriting existence. Equally predictably, by young adulthood Patience left the restrictions of home in search of a new life in Philadelphia. By her early twenties, she had married an ageing but wealthy barrel maker named Joseph Wright, making no secret among her friends of the lack of ardour she felt towards him.

Ardour or not, when Wright died in 1769, Patience had four children and was pregnant with her fifth. Her husband had made no provision for his wife and children in his will: though she was able to retain their marital home in Bordentown, New Jersey, she was prevented by law from inheriting the rest of his estate, leaving her penniless and without income. She needed a new plan.

There were very few income streams open to the women of New England in 1769; instead of taking in lodgers or laundry, Patience and her sister, now also widowed, made a remarkable, entrepreneurial move. Drawing upon the skills they had honed through their childhoods, they set up a waxworks, modelling busts so life-like visitors were fooled into striking up conversations with them. When Wright sculpted, she did so with a vigour not often exhibited in public by women on either side of the Atlantic, working with energy and passion, holding the bust in her lap and shielding it from her sitter with her skirts, where she could keep the wax warm and pliable. The sisters' collection of waxwork models grew in number and within a few years was sufficient to open a House of Wax, receiving growing numbers of paying guests, first in Philadelphia and swiftly afterwards in Manhattan. But when a fire swept through the Manhattan block in June 1771, destroying the sisters' entire stock, the indomitable Patience Wright set off on a brave new path, one which took her all the way to a 'handsome House' just off the Strand.

At first, London didn't quite know how to take her. She did everything English women were raised not to do: she talked – incessantly and somewhat coarsely; she greeted strangers as old friends, kissing every American she encountered; and she seemed to embrace intrigue for its own sake. Disarmingly open, honest and friendly, Patience yelled out of windows to attract the attention of passers-by, talked the straight talk of the New World, and made an entrance wherever she went with her sallow face and wooden shoes. And naturally, she worked her magic, crafting unnervingly life-like busts in a medium that was entirely new to the English. And so, very quickly, London came to love her.

Within a year, she was in huge demand, sculpting increasingly lofty heads. William Pitt, Earl of Chatham, became one of Wright's biggest fans (she adored him in return, championing him as America's 'Guardian Angel'). Before long, she found herself the recipient of an audience with George III and Queen Charlotte, whom she threw entirely off-kilter by addressing them as 'George' and 'Charlotte'. In just a few short years, Wright made an astonishing leap from penniless widow with five children to support to New York entrepreneur, to hostess of the British peerage. Number 30, Suffolk Street began to fill with her wax figures, and so she opened her home as a House of Wax. The wife of American ambassador John Adams was among her visitors and recalled having been fooled for ten minutes into believing that 'an old clergyman sitting reading the paper in the middle of the room' was real, before finally being told he was in fact made of wax. There can be no doubt of Wright's skill: her one surviving piece stands in a corner of Westminster Abbey museum to this day, the figure of William Pitt, made after his death. Its quality bears testament to her artistry; it's easy to see why her eighteenth-century audience were so commonly fooled into trying to make small talk with her sculptures.

The medium and manner in which she worked, clasping her pieces between her thighs and bringing them to full colour unthinkably, with ingredients such as tobacco spittle, were out of step with eighteenth-century sensibilities. Add to this Wright's disarming manner and her easy disregard for social convention, and the impact cannot be underestimated. Her sitters were thrown off guard, an experience they seem to have found at once unnerving and seductive. Having sculpted the busts of the Royals, a sitting with Patience Wright became entirely *de rigueur* and by the mid 1770s, her name was rarely out of the newspapers.

In spite of it all, London ways didn't rub off on her: she continued to embrace everyone with a kiss to both cheeks, to address them by their Christian names, and to make no distinction between classes. To her contemporaries she was in every sense a New Englander, with all the characteristic forthright candour that was starting to emerge in colonists across the Atlantic; seen through a twenty-first century lens, however, she was every bit the spirited, straight-talking New Yorker.

In the main, her sitters found the cumulative experience of being in her presence so beguiling, they began to talk unguardedly. Wright began to piece together details about the movements of leading politicians who sat for her; equally, their wives spoke with indiscretion about their husbands' views on developments in the American colony, and steadily, Wright began to build a picture of those who were more likely to support the colony's calls for independence. As revolution in America drew nearer, it occurred to her that the information her clients shared might be of significant use to those back home. And so, sculptor turned spy, she began to smuggle intelligence back to Benjamin Franklin via her sister Rachel in Philadelphia, hidden within buttons on the wax models she shipped home.

Once war broke out, Wright threw open the doors of 30 Suffolk Street to American prisoners of war and made no secret where her allegiances lay. That same untamed and free-talking nature which had first won her the patronage of the British high aristocracy was now also her undoing. Her name appeared less and less in the London press, she began to lose her clientele and with it, her livelihood.

Her adulation for Benjamin Franklin remained a constant through these years; in fact, to the modern eye, it appeared now to tip over into something approaching obsession. Private correspondence reveals letter after letter from Wright to Franklin, increasingly without response. With the colony fighting for independence, Franklin no doubt had more pressing things on his mind, but the longer he ignored her letters, the harder she tried to gain his attention. Her letters grew wilder: she even suggested he should start a revolution on English soil, taking the downtrodden people of England with him to victory against the evils of the Establishment. Franklin ignored that one, too.

She tried, briefly, to turn her fortunes around in Paris, but returned to London in the 1780s and instead threw her energy into attempting to secure a sitting with George Washington himself, and with it, a passage home. In 1786, just as she finally received the news she had wanted from Washington, Wright took a fall and died suddenly. Her sister Rachel persisted in efforts to secure the financial support of her former patrons, including Franklin, so that Patience's remains could be shipped back to America for burial. Tragically, no one came to her aid, and Wright was buried in London, whereabouts unknown; the grave has been lost and was almost certainly unmarked.

Patience Wright was the first American woman ever to earn her living as a sculptor. She was also a force of nature who swept through London in the 1770s, turning convention on its head and seducing respectable society in a way no woman had quite done before. Disinterested in gender or class restrictions, she allowed herself to be led by her own zeal, driven to build a life for herself and her children on her own terms. Her political convictions, too, came from a place of passion: though she spent the last years of her life in London, she was every bit an American and seized every opportunity to celebrate her homeland, even scolding George III himself for his stance on America, much to his bewilderment.

At the heart of her remarkable artistry was her capacity to disarm her sitters just enough to catch their spirit in the wax she cradled between her thighs. As an artist, she was described by contemporaries as 'extraordinary', 'ingenious' and 'perfection'. As a woman, she was a fervent, untamed spirit, labelled by an uneasy London as 'Promethean' in her fearless vigour. A powerhouse, entirely out of her time, for which she is commemorated.

3 BRYANSTON STREET, MARYLEBONE

Today, 3 Bryanston Street is occupied by a multi-storey car park but in the 1820s, Bryanston Street was a smart address in the heart of the capital. Number 3 was home to Roderick Impey Murchison, a wealthy Scot who had fought in the Napoleonic Wars and thereafter became a keen and noteworthy amateur geologist, and his wife Charlotte, who encouraged, participated in and later financed his scientific endeavours. Charlotte was on the brink of inheriting a considerable fortune, which would see them move to an enviable home in fashionable Belgravia, one large enough to host parties for several hundred guests, served by a significant staff. For now, however, Bryanston Street was home, positioned across the street from a grandiose early Georgian mansion, now the DoubleTree hotel, first built for a lady-in-waiting at the court of George II.

In July 1829, the Murchisons welcomed an unlikely houseguest. They were already well acquainted with the woman who arrived dressed in the modest garb of a hard-working Dissenting Christian. Her only formal education had been at Sunday School and she spoke with a strong Dorset accent, paying little heed to grammar. To all the world she must have seemed an unlikely parlour companion for Charlotte Murchison and yet the three were close and easy company. Moreover, the Murchisons had come to depend on the vast, self-taught expertise and growing international reputation of their unlikely friend, who would come to affect the course of scientific understanding of the early origins of life on the planet.

MARY ANNING
(1799–1847)

In the early decades of the nineteenth century the finest scientific minds overwhelmingly adhered to the Biblical version of the Earth's early origins: the many species within God's creation were constants, created during Genesis, saved from the flood by Noah. Darwin wouldn't create a storm with his *Origin of Species* until 1859: in the 1820s, the concept of 'extinction' was just as absent from scientific debate as was 'evolution'. But in 1812, more than forty-five years before Darwin went public with his theory, an uneducated and poverty-stricken 13-year-old girl from Lyme Regis named Mary Anning had made a discovery that changed everything: the first complete fossilised remains of an Ichthyosaur.

Anning's finds initially represented little more than an income stream for her family, brought to the brink of destitution after the death of her father, Richard. But her passion grew along with her expertise. It was to be the start of a groundbreaking career in fossil hunting for Anning that would unearth several new species, help launch the careers of several (male) geologists, and, crucially, lay the foundations for Darwin's thesis.

The Ichthyosaur was bought by the lord of a nearby manor house

for £23, who sold it on to a collector in London. The scientific community pounced on the find: references to it cropped up in lectures
and in scientific papers. At no point, however, was Anning credited
with its discovery. This was to be a recurring theme throughout
her career: although her body of finds amounts to one of the most
important in the history of palaeontology, her name was routinely
absent in any ensuing discussions. Several of the male geologists
who came to own and study her finds had new species named after
them; in her lifetime, not a single British geologist named one of her
finds after her.

Anning risked her life throughout the winter months when storms
battered the fragile cliffs of Lyme, causing rock-fall that would reveal
new specimens. In 1823, she discovered the first complete Plesiosaurus
and five years later, the first pterosaur to have been found in the UK.
Her finds, and their subsequent sales, earned her enough to finance
the purchase of her own glass-fronted shop in Lyme Regis in 1827.
Anning's Fossil Depot was soon frequented by visitors from around the
globe, including, in 1844, King Frederick Augustus II of Saxony.

In 1825, the Murchisons from London, both keen amateur geologists, arrived in Lyme Regis to break an expedition along the south
coast. Charlotte Murchison decided she should remain in the town
a while alone, keen to learn from Anning, of whom they had heard
much talk. The two women were from entirely different worlds but,
with a shared passion for the secrets held within the rocks, they
became firm friends and after Charlotte's first sojourn in Lyme
Regis, corresponded throughout their lives. In the summer of 1829,
at the request of the Murchisons, Anning came to stay at the house
on Bryanston Street, to visit the resting place of her Plesiosaurus,
which she had unearthed in 1823. This was the Geological Society
at Somerset House, where a consternation had ensued when the
Plesiosaurus proved too large to be manoeuvred around the stair-
well. It was the only occasion in Anning's life that saw her leave
Lyme Regis and she made the most of it, taking in the museum
owned by her agent, collector George Brettingham Sowerby, just off

Covent Garden, as well as the British Museum, the zoological gardens and the newly built and incredibly elegant Regent Street, the details recorded eagerly in her diary.

The impact of her life's work on the science of geology, and in particular on palaeontology, both of which were in their infancy in the early nineteenth century, cannot be underestimated. It was her experience and inquisitive mind that first alerted her to the true nature of the strange stones she often discovered within the abdominal cavity of the remains of entire specimens. Within the stones she found fish bones, scales and other small bones, and came to realise they were fossilised faeces. She called them coprolite and further study, undertaken by Anning and her friend, geologist William Buckland, enabled them to uncover a clear food chain and to unveil ancient ecosystems.

Roderick Murchison, who credited Anning for helping his wife Charlotte to ensure 'my first collection was much enriched', became a leading geologist in his own right. William Buckland, too, was widely celebrated within his lifetime, and was largely credited solo for his work on coprolites and food chains, though he did acknowledge Anning's central role when addressing the Geological Society on the subject in 1829. Anning won lifelong friendship from the geologists with whom she worked, but within her lifetime, her central role in the important discoveries she made all too often went without credit. When she died at the age of forty-seven, the President of the Geological Society delivered a eulogy, the first ever delivered for a woman by the Society, acknowledging the considerable impact of her work on their body of knowledge.

In fact, recent commentators have gone further still, asserting that the collected fossil finds of Mary Anning amount to the most significant of all time. Mary Anning died of breast cancer, dependent on the financial support of her friends and without ever having received official acknowledgement of her groundbreaking work. Her unstinting dedication to the field had nonetheless facilitated the careers of several leading male geologists with whom she collaborated, not least of which was Roderick Murchison. Crucially, Anning's work provided an evidence-base for a sea-change in scientific theory about extinction and evolution, and was to scaffold the emerging science of palaeontology.

5 BLANDFORD SQUARE, MARYLEBONE

In the mid decades of the nineteenth century, Blandford Square sat nestled in the spot where St Marylebone meets Lisson Grove, a comfortable, middle-class enclave, described in the London Gazette *of 1834 as 'one of the most splendid portions of the metropolis'. Today, much of the square, and all of neighbouring Harewood Square has gone, lost in 1899 to the construction of Marylebone Station. Only a single strip of terraced houses remains of Blandford Square, along with the Convent of the Sisters of Mercy on Harewood Avenue, which once dominated the square. But in the early decades of the nineteenth century, the area attracted a number of the capital's most significant creatives, including novelists George Eliot, who lived at number 16, and Wilkie Collins, who briefly lived at number 38. George Hayter, painter of miniatures for the Royal household, was also a resident, and sculptor John Graham Lough lived on the neighbouring Harewood Square. At number 5, reached by a flight of steps from pavement level to imposing double doors beneath a fanlight window, lived the remarkable family of the former Radical abolitionist MP, William Smith, now ageing and resident with his son, Benjamin Leigh Smith, also a Radical MP. On his death in 1860, Benjamin bequeathed the house to his daughter, Barbara, who was already on a path that would help change the lives of the women of Britain.*

BARBARA LEIGH SMITH BODICHON
(1827–91)

Barbara Leigh Smith Bodichon was every bit a Pre-Raphaelite woman – a celebrated watercolour artist in her own right, she was a close friend of William Morris, George Eliot, Dante Gabriel Rossetti and his wife and muse, Elizabeth Siddal. She was first cousin to Florence Nightingale and her brother, Benjamin, was an Arctic explorer, responsible among other things for bringing live polar bears to London Zoo.

But her life had none of the languor of Siddal, for instance, as encapsulated in some of Rossetti's most enduring masterpieces. Bodichon was a game-changer, once writing in a letter to a relative, 'I am one of the cracked people of the world, and I like to herd with the cracked,' adding that she was 'never happy in an English genteel life'.

She had not been raised within the cosy convention of the genteel. Her father, Radical MP, Benjamin Leigh Smith, and her mother, Charlotte, chose not to marry, though they remained lifelong partners and raised five children together. Barbara and her four siblings were educated at a local school, alongside working-class children, and when they reached the age of twenty-one, their father endowed each of them with a generous annual allowance, regardless of gender. Barbara embarked upon adulthood with a passion for art, a strident sense of the need for gender equality, and the financial liberty to be able to work to put it right.

In her youth, she travelled widely, making treks with close female companions, unaccompanied by male chaperons, climbing mountains in pantaloons and wading through streams in a state of semi-undress. She studied art under William Holman Hunt and would in time be exhibited at the Royal Academy. As a young woman, she fell in love with John Chapman, editor of the *Westminster Review*, but was so philosophically opposed to marriage, given the immediate loss of a married woman's property to her husband, and the gender imbalance inherent within the divorce laws of the day, she refused his proposal. When finally she did marry, to a suitably progressively inclined French doctor named Eugene Bodichon, it was in 1857: the same year the Matrimonial Causes Act brought about new legal rights for married women.

Her passion for the betterment of the role of women grew and she found common cause with a group of feminists, journalists and benefactors in London who decided to organise themselves, calling themselves the Langham Place Group. The Ladies of Langham Place established their base along the lines of a gentleman's club, with a coffee shop, meeting rooms and a reading room. Except, of course, that the clientele was exclusively female. The group turned a spotlight on what they considered to be four fundamental rights which needed to be asserted for the women of Britain in order to ensure true equality: the right to vote, the right to access education, the right to work and keep one's wages, and the right to retain one's legal identity and property within marriage. Barbara Leigh Smith Bodichon, far from being 'cracked', used her wit, passion, vigour and charisma to help found the country's first women's equality movement.

In the early 1850s, she began researching primary schools across the capital and worked with an educator to come up with a new, more enlightened model. The result was the Portman Hall School in Paddington, which opened in 1852: a progressive, nondenominational establishment that would give equal opportunities to children of both genders and of all social classes. She was uneasy, too, about the closed doors women encountered in the world of university education. Working with Emily Davies, she was instrumental in establishing Girton College, Cambridge, which in 1866 became the country's first residential college for women enabling degree-level studies. She gave generously of both her time and her funds. Interviews for the teaching staff were held at her home on Blandford Square, and the first five women to study at Girton would become regular guests at her Sussex home.

In 1854, Bodichon's *Brief Summary in Plain Language of the Most Important Laws Concerning Women* laid the foundations for a groundswell campaign which would finally culminate in the Married Women's Property Act of 1870, giving women the legal right to maintain their own private income and property within marriage. The Langham Place Group launched the *English Women's Journal* in 1858, steered by Bodichon, to raise the profile of their campaign. The same year, Bodichon published *Women and Work*, asserting that women's financial dependence on a man within marriage was degrading. By 1866, the year Girton College opened, she and the Langham Place Group turned their attention to a new campaign: the vote, gathering to form the first women's suffrage movement in Britain.

Bodichon lived a remarkable life, so diverse in her passions, causes and achievements that they are challenging to document: responsible for a sea-change in the way in which women were perceived by society and by law, and yet largely forgotten on the pages of our history books.

PORTMAN SQUARE, WIGMORE STREET, MARYLEBONE

Lower Seymour Street, later renamed Wigmore Street, as it appeared in the 1850s is still partly in evidence today, a short row of dark red-brick terraced homes that sit between Portman Square and Great Cumberland Place, with their stable and coach provision in the adjoining street, Berkeley Mews. In 1858 the Samaritans Hospital for Women moved into the south side of the street, causing some consternation by erecting huge boards which covered the entirety of the front face of the building, emboldened with foot-high lettering detailing the many gynaecological complaints the hospital catered to. Pioneering medicine it may have been, but to the genteel residents of Lower Seymour Street, it was vulgar and distasteful. In the same year the hospital's near-neighbours at number 5 welcomed their fourth child, a daughter; the house no longer stands, but the infant born at number 5 in 1858 would become a pioneer of women in music and one of the era's most significant composers.

ETHEL SMYTH
(1858–1944)

On an autumnal morning in 1902, a spirited 44-year-old Englishwoman stepped off the boat train in Paris. Dressed in her habitual tweed, and with a hat more than likely fixed a little crooked in her hair (as she once confessed was often the case), she had more pressing things on her mind than the paraphernalia of fashion. She was a woman with impressive aristocratic connections, but was disinterested in conventional sensibilities. It was seven in the morning and she had just four hours before making the return journey home. She waited until a more respectable eight o'clock before putting in a telephone call to the Parisian hotel at which an American impresario named Maurice Grau was staying, begging that he meet with her that morning.

By the time the woman boarded the eleven o'clock train bound for home, Grau had scanned the score she had handed him for her stage opera, *Der Wald*; studied the array of newspaper clippings and box-office takings from the production's record-breaking London premiere and handed over a signed contract for a performance at the Metropolitan Opera, which he scheduled for the following March.

It had been a tenacious move which flew in the face of convention: at the turn of the century, respectable women generally didn't travel without a chaperone and certainly didn't pursue their personal ambitions quite so pluckily. But then neither did women take up a career in musical composition; those few who did generally composed for the drawing room, never for something as gutsy as opera.

Ethel Smyth wasn't interested in convention. She had been born to a major-general in the Bengal Army, raised in a wealthy, well-connected home by an increasingly distant mother who claimed the Empress Eugénie, wife of Napoleon III, as a neighbour and friend. She knew the restrictions placed on women of the late-Victorian era all too well. As a young woman, she had successfully battled with her father, John Hall Smyth, for permission to study composition at the Leipzig Conservatoire. She became closely acquainted with Clara Schumann, a leading pianist of the Romantic era, and through her, with composers such as Brahms, Grieg, Tchaikovsky and Dvořák. She already had an impressive oeuvre behind her by 1902, but yearned to be heard in America (*see Appendix, page 163*).

In the event, *Der Wald* broke the five-figure mark at the Metropolitan Opera on its opening night, the only production to have done so that season, and was met with a sustained standing ovation. The critics were lukewarm at best, but Smyth was used to reviews which were more concerned with analysing whether her femininity was brought to the fore in her work, or whether it showed an unbecoming masculinity, than giving any real consideration to its inherent worth. In any case, she told the press she was far more interested in whether the piece was a popular success: 'I care more for the opinion of the people in the galleries than for the opinion of any other public.'

Of greater significance, hers was to be the only opera composed by a woman staged at the Metropolitan for more than a century to follow. Recognition was slower to come in her homeland: though well-connected, Smyth was always open about her sexuality, publishing honest memoirs about her love affairs with women. By 1910, she had become a dedicated militant suffragette, participating in a mass stone-throwing exercise with Emmeline Pankhurst, with whom she is believed to have had a sustained affair and alongside whom she was imprisoned for a two-month spell at Holloway in 1912. The previous year, she stood with the Women's Social and Political Union in boycotting the 1911 census, scoring her entry with the words, 'No Vote, No Census'. That same year, she composed what would soon be taken up as the suffrage movement's anthem, 'The March of the Women', which she famously conducted with her toothbrush from between the bars of her Holloway cell, while the hundred or so fellow suffragists imprisoned with her marched and sang in the square yard below.

Despite having raged against the British establishment, when war broke out in 1914, Smyth was quick to step up and do her bit, training as a radiographer and volunteering in military hospitals on the continent, as well as working as an interpreter for the British Army in Italy. Though war stemmed her capacity to compose, she discovered an ability to write prose and embarked upon a series of ten largely autobiographical novels and memoirs, the writing of which was met with the disapproval of Pankhurst, but which latterly brought her into close friendship with Virginia Woolf, with whom she fell in love at the age of seventy-one.

Recognition for her services to music came in 1922 in the form of a Damehood, the first woman ever awarded a DBE for musical composition. Then in 1934, at the age of seventy-five and by now having entirely lost her hearing, Britain finally celebrated her considerable body of work at the Royal Albert Hall.

Ethel Smyth is remembered for her fearless disregard for gender-restrictive convention, and her defiant determination to dedi-cate her life openly and in plain sight to her music, her sexuality and her political convictions.

17 NOTTINGHAM PLACE, MARYLEBONE

By the early decades of the twentieth century, Marylebone's Nottingham Place was a sedate, unassuming street. Its early days at the turn of the eighteenth century, when it had been one of London's most 'airy and fashionable' addresses, had given way to a succession of hard-working professionals by the late Victorian period. Many of them were medics, including the trailblazing medical pioneer Sophia Jex-Blake. By 1911, the census listed a sole occupant living within the twenty rooms of number 17 along with a domestic staff of four – a cook, a parlourmaid, a housemaid and an under-housemaid. Nestled among the street's boarding houses and nursing homes, it was a fittingly unostentatious address for one of London's most self-effacing and widely respected surgeons, Louisa Aldrich-Blake.

LOUISA ALDRICH-BLAKE

(1865–1925)

Often, the conscientious, the meticulous, the unerringly reliable are not given to self-promotion, and yet their dedication to a life well lived can leave behind a legacy worthy of celebrating. Louisa Aldrich-Blake, Britain's first female surgeon, left just such a legacy.

In the mid-1890s, when Louisa Aldrich-Blake first arrived in London, she was a studious, shy and self-contained young woman in her mid-twenties, from rural Monmouthshire. The daughter of a rector, she had been largely home-educated and life in the nation's capital would have presented her with quite a contrast to the one she had known at the Rectory. All who would come to know her were clear, however: shy she may have been, but retiring she was not. She enrolled at Hampstead's Royal Free Hospital School of Medicine for Women and from the start had her sights set on a career in surgery.

Louisa Aldrich-Blake was joining medical school at a time when the presence of women in the profession was new enough to be regarded with widespread mistrust. Her contemporary, Maud Chadburn, a fellow surgeon and founder of the South London Hospital for Women and Children, would later recall that Aldrich-Blake had been able to withstand the 'jars' of opposition to her presence in an overwhelmingly male world with considerable grace, in equal part thanks to the quality of her work and her 'serenity, equanimity and self-reliance'. Chadburn lauded her friend and colleague for the 'excellence of her doing', describing her as 'not a fighting pioneer', of the likes of Jex-Blake and Garrett Anderson, but rather 'a necessary sequence' to their kind; a consummate professional who demonstrated the value of women in medicine with everything she undertook.

Louisa Aldrich-Blake began her surgical career at the Elizabeth Garrett Anderson Hospital in 1885, and was promoted to full surgeon in 1905. She later went on to become the first female surgical registrar, anaesthetist and lecturer on anaesthetics at the Royal Free Hospital in Hampstead. By 1914 she was already established as an accomplished surgeon, but the outbreak of the First World War presented an enormous opportunity to make a real difference.

From the earliest months of the war, Aldrich-Blake threw herself into serving. She worked double duties at the Royal Free, covering for absent male surgeons, and used all her leave to travel to Belgium and France, volunteering in military hospitals so as to enable serving British Army surgeons to take leave themselves. This relentless pace she maintained throughout the war, until 1919, when those enlisted began to return home.

Prior to the war, hospital archives suggest her influence in London hospitals had been restricted to surgical procedures on women and children; female surgeons were not encouraged to operate on men. The war, however, created a dearth of male surgeons at the same time as it vastly increased the number of men needing surgery. Her experience in British Army hospitals on the Western Front made clear to her the mounting crisis in medical personnel. In May 1916, she seized the initiative. If women were stepping up to plug the gaps in factories and farms, why not also in the Royal Army Medical Corps? Louisa contacted all women on the Medical Register, making a personal plea for them to serve. A remarkable forty-eight women medics were subsequently enrolled, the first thirty-eight being deployed to Malta and the Eastern Front by August 1916. By October 1916, the War Office asked Louisa to recruit a further fifty women medics, which she achieved within a matter of weeks by appealing directly to all those who had recently qualified.

The momentum of women in medicine, and particularly in surgery, gathered apace after the war. Louisa became the Royal Free Hospital's first female consultant surgeon, a role in which she would continue until a month before her death. Her work on the operating table was widely admired by her colleagues, with Chadburn describing her as a 'bold, courageous, level-headed' surgeon, with hands so deft at their work that 'her finger-tips obviously carried brains in them'. Later in her career, Louisa pioneered surgical procedures in the treatment of rectal and cervical cancers and was made Dame Aldrich-Blake in the 1925 New Year's Honours List.

Throughout her career she remained disinterested in personal distinction, reticent and self-contained socially and yet widely lauded as wholly dedicated to her profession, to her hospital and unfailingly generous and accessible to colleagues, juniors and students. Louisa Aldrich-Blake's energy, her spotless reputation for bold, meticulous and pioneering surgery, and her career-long value as a generous colleague and mentor proved a real force for change. Her legacy helped transform the presence of women in medicine from something merely permissible by law but barely tolerated to something altogether more valued.

32 RANSTON STREET, MARYLEBONE

Charles Street lay at the heart of one of the most heavily deprived areas of Victorian Marylebone. The slum housing that still lined the street in 1885 was razed, rebuilt and renamed Ranston Street in the last years of the century, although the ghost of its earlier incarnation lives on in the narrow, cobbled road surface which has survived to this day. In the first half of the century surveys into housing conditions across Marylebone painted a grim picture of the street, with many extended family groups living in unsanitary conditions and often in cramped, single rooms. Alcohol con-sumption was high in areas of urban deprivation like this: home offered no comfort, ale houses were just around every corner and provided the only viable environment in which to fill the scant time between work and sleep. By the late nineteenth century, Charles Street had one of the highest mor-tality rates in Marylebone, and the Armstrong family were typical of its residents. Charles Armstrong and his family lived at number 32. He was a chimney sweep and his extended family lived alongside him and on neigh-bouring streets. His wife gained a reputation for heavy drinking and times were tough. So in 1885, when Elizabeth Armstrong received an offer with significant financial recompense, she chose not to refuse. In a moment, the life of her young daughter, Eliza, took a turn that would reverberate around the world, leaving an indelible legacy.

ELIZA ARMSTRONG
(1872–1938)

In 1885, a deal was struck between the owner of the sensationalist newspaper, the *Pall Mall Gazette*, and the mother of 13-year-old Eliza Armstrong. Eliza was not party to the negotiation, it was presented to her as a *fait accompli*. It was a moment which would briefly make Eliza a household name but which would subsequently alter British child protection laws for good. The newspaper man was W. T. Stead, Victorian Britain's first truly investigative journalist. Together with the head of the Salvation Army, Bramwell Booth, Stead had concocted a scheme with which to spotlight the rampant and illicit trade of send-ing British children to European brothels.

Working via a reluctant, reformed former brothel keeper who had sought solace with the Salvation Army, Stead bought Eliza from her alcoholic mother for £5, convincing Eliza (though not her mother) that she was entering into domestic service. In 1885, £5 was the equivalent of around £600, according to the Bank of England inflation calcula-tor. For a family in desperate living conditions, this was sizeable sum, almost certainly the best part of a year's rent, and came with the added benefit that there would be one less mouth to feed.

Eliza's life, however, was about to take a terrifying turn. Upon leaving her home, she was drugged with chloroform and taken to an abortionist so that her virginity could be verified. Later, she awoke in a brothel, in the company of a heavily inebriated man: Stead. Although a lifelong teetotaller, he had steeled himself to carry out the sham *almost* in full, and had needed the contents of a bottle of champagne in order to do so. Eliza screamed in terror and Stead left. From the brothel, Eliza was taken overnight to the home of another stranger, this time, surgeon Robert Romley Cheyne, who lived just off Marylebone High Street in the unfashionable but solidly respectable Nottingham Place. Here, she would have been looked after, although she could hardly have known that for sure, given what she had just been through. Early the following morning, Booth and others of Stead's associates returned to carry her off to France.

Eliza's kidnapping was only the first stage of Stead's plan. He had wanted to demonstrate how easily a child could be abducted from her home and smuggled out of the country without coming to the attention of the authorities. Once this exercise was completed, he needed to go public. Eliza's traumatic ordeal was to be serialised in Stead's newspaper in four instalments entitled *The Maiden Tribute of Modern Babylon*. The week before its publication, he cannily warned his readers:

All those who are squeamish, and all those who are prudish, and all those who would prefer to live in a fool's paradise of imaginary innocence and purity, selfishly oblivious to the horrible realities which torment those whose lives are passed in the London inferno, will do well not to read the Pall Mall Gazette *of Monday and the three following days.*[1]

Stead left his readership in no doubt that the wholesale trade in British children to the pleasure palaces of continental Europe was a national

---

[1] *The Pall Mall Gazette*, Saturday 4 July 1885. The full text of 'The Maiden Tribute of Modern Babylon' is available on www.attackingthedevil.co.uk, the W. T. Stead Resource Site.

scourge, taking place on a vast scale. By the time the final instalment of the newspaper went to press, copies were passing hands for ten times their street value. Thousands descended in protest on the capital, including wagonloads of virgins dressed in white, calling for the House of Commons to pass the much-stalled Criminal Law Amendment Bill, which would raise the age of consent from thirteen to sixteen.

Stead and Bramwell Booth stood trial; they had, after all, brought about the unlawful kidnapping of a child, and enabled her sexual assault at the hands of an insalubrious midwife. To add to her ordeal, Eliza was further called upon to give evidence at the Old Bailey; a trial indeed for a poorly educated girl from Marylebone. Stead served three months with hard labour but carried his sentence as a badge of pride, marking the anniversary of his imprisonment annually by turning up to work in his prison uniform. He would eventually end his days on board RMS *Titanic*.

In time, the spotlight faded on the 13-year-old innocent whose childhood was ripped apart to force the world to face injustice. After the trial, she was sent to a residential school in Essex to be prepared for a life in domestic service, later working as a nursemaid for a family in the North East. In due course, she married, was twice widowed and lived out the rest of her days with her six children. As far as records indicate, she never returned to London.

It's easy to judge Elizabeth Armstrong's actions through a twenty-first century lens, but harder to assess the extent to which her neighbours in and around Charles Street reacted when the case became the talk of the city. Like many on the street, the Armstrong family were struggling to cope when Stead made his lucrative offer. Life was tougher and shorter then: this was an era in which unwanted infants were reported every week in the press having been found abandoned under railway arches all over the city, or advertised for in the 'Wanted' columns by insalubrious baby farmers, fostering and adopting for cash on the black market. Elizabeth Armstrong wasn't the only mother in the city prepared to sacrifice one child to ease the burden of raising another. However, the tide was beginning to turn;

the NSPCC had been established as a London-based organisation in 1884. The nation had been rocked by several high-profile baby farmer cases which had culminated at the gallows. The notion of child protection was just starting to formulate, and London was beginning to look differently at cases such as these.

Certainly, there is some evidence to suggest the Armstrongs' neighbours might have taken a hard line on the choice Elizabeth made. Trouble brewed for the family in the years after the trial. In 1886 Charles Armstrong was found guilty of assaulting a neighbour after a fracas, and two years later, Elizabeth was also imprisoned for assault while drunk and disorderly. At her trial, her defence cited the sustained trouble the family had been subjected to locally since Eliza's case and revealed that Charles had buckled under the strain and had recently been declared insane. He was incarcerated at the infamous Colney Hatch Lunatic Asylum, his records showing he had been hearing voices, and would die there in 1890. Amid the alcohol, street brawls and criminal court proceedings, it's little wonder that Eliza's brothers, John and Charles, also had brushes with the law, resulting in John being sent to the workhouse and Charles being detained at an Industrial School, where conditions were typically harsh and perilous.

Eliza once wrote that she bore Stead no ill; she had been an unwitting and unwilling party to the traumas inflicted upon her; bore with dignity the further trauma of the witness stand and sacrificed her privacy so that her story could act as a catalyst for change on a national scale. Her former home in the slums of Marylebone may have long since disappeared, and her legacy lives on in our statute books, but while the history books record Stead's part in the change to the child protection law, Eliza's contribution was never formally acknowledged – until now.

2 SPRINGFIELD ROAD, MARYLEBONE
In the 1920s, after the First World War, number 2, Springfield Road, Marylebone was divided into three flats, each unremarkable in size or

architecture. Inside, however, one of the apartments was highly distinct from its neighbours: the 25-year-old single female occupant had powered the entire space with electricity, wiring it herself as a means of ensuring adequate lighting. She discovered something else in the process: electricity saved time, bought her a little freedom from the laborious business of heating a home with coal and cleaning everything by hand. Already she was a supporter of women's suffrage, but electricity, she realised, brought with it another kind of emancipation, one that was every bit as essential as the vote if women were to have a real chance at equality: freedom from 'domestic drudgery'. The pursuit of electrical engineering in the name of gender equality was to become a driving force in the remarkable career of Caroline Harriet Haslett.

CAROLINE HARRIET HASLETT
(1895–1957)

Caroline Haslett was of good birth. Not in the sense of class, wealth or status: her father was a railway engineer and her mother worked hard to tend to her family of five children. But the Haslett household was nonetheless an enlightened one. When as a young girl Caroline began to rebel against the expectation to help her mother with the household chores, she was allowed instead to indulge her love of tools, learning how to help her father in his workshop. She did join her mother, but it was in the active pursuit of female suffrage, not in the kitchen or scullery, with the tacit approval of her father. And when ill-health kept Caroline off school for extended periods, her family encouraged her to persevere and complete her education, ignoring the advice of her head teacher, who suggested further studies would prove 'pointless'.

In fact, Haslett's life and work was to prove far from pointless, something she delighted in inviting her old head to help her celebrate periodically. During the First World War, she took up employment as a secretary with a large engineering firm, the Cochran Boiler Company. Her considerable interest in engineering soon became evident, and she was given basic training in London and at the company's plant in Annan, Scotland, initially to the consternation of her male colleagues, but soon proved herself a capable and charismatic match. In 1918, she was asked to run the firm's London office.

Her passion for engineering grew into something of a crusade, as she began to see the potential of technological advancements for liberating ordinary women from full-time domestic servitude. Wiring her own Marylebone apartment with electricity (still far from commonplace in 1920s households) opened her eyes to its very real impact on quality of life: adequate lighting alone, she later argued, changed everything in a home and shouldn't be underestimated.

A committed feminist, Haslett soon came to see that true emancipation for women would require not only a vote, but freedom from household chores, and she saw the widespread availability of electricity, along with an education for girls which included science, as the surest route to bringing about that freedom. An advertisement in *Engineering* magazine in 1919 gave her precisely the vehicle within which she could pursue these goals. It read:

> *Required, Lady with some experience in Engineering Works, as Organising Secretary for a Women's Engineering Society.*

She brought to the role not only her passion for engineering, but also a significant, visionary intellect, a capacity to organise, recruit and educate, and a charismatic presence. The appointment came at a crucial time for women in industry: the Restoration of Pre-War Practices Act of 1919 saw many thousands of women dismissed from their wartime jobs, especially in engineering. Tension towards those women who stood their ground was high. Against this backdrop, Haslett became a significant voice in the struggle not only to keep women in engineering, but to encourage more to train. The WES openly invited women who cared about their continued capacity to work in the industry to join their ranks so as to help safeguard women's interests. Meanwhile, Haslett spoke at international engineering conventions, wrote extensively in periodicals and newspapers and published several of her own books.

Her personal correspondence reveals the extent to which she was blazing a trail in this respect: she recounts having to convince door-men at length that she was indeed on the official guest list for the otherwise all-male annual engineering convention. In 1925, a friend wrote to Haslett asking for advice on how to conduct herself, introduce herself and even what she should wear at a forthcoming conference. 'Please tell me,' she wrote, 'am I a lady or an engineer?' Her friend had constructed herself a hat especially – her father's top hat, embellished with some ribbon and frill, 'to give it the hybrid semi feminine air'. In response, Haslett was emphatic: 'we are going as engineers and not as wives'. As for the hat, she wasn't impressed. Its description alone, she said, 'increases my alarm and anxiety'. Her words and opinions flow freely and even now seem harsh in places, but have to be taken in the context of the widespread malaise about her career choices. In her biography, Haslett's sister, Rosalind Messenger, noted that even the prominent suffragette, Emmeline Pankhurst, reacted with undis-guised shock when Haslett told her how she earned her living – 'But surely, that's a very unsuitable occupation for a lady, isn't it?'

In the interwar years, changing public perceptions towards women in engineering proved a mammoth task, but it was one to which Haslett's unshakeable passion, professionalism and charisma was well suited. In 1924, she headed a new organisation, the Electrical Association for Women, established with the specific purpose of spreading confidence among ordinary women about electricity in the home, emboldened by its slogan, 'Emancipation from Drudgery'. It struck a chord with thousands of women for whom a return to domes-tic service, or worse, being once more confined to the home without work was a bitter pill after their service during the war years.

Haslett's reputation and influence grew at home and abroad. She travelled widely, speaking about the role of women in engineering and about her commitment to bringing electricity to ordinary homes. On her travels, she met some of the leading scientists and engineers of the day, figures such as Albert Einstein and Henry Ford. Her cha-risma and conviction garnered support wherever she went and she often spoke openly about her belief that the best brains in science and engineering were the worst possible voices to light a spark in the minds of young women: women needed to hear real women, talking about engineering in plain language, she said, if they were to be enticed in. By the Second World War, her reputation had grown significantly and she was called upon to act as government advisor on issues relating to engineering. In 1947 she became the first woman appointed to sit on the British Electricity Authority, becoming a Dame in the same year.

By the 1950s, the London electoral roll shows that Haslett no longer resided at her self-wired apartment on Springfield Road, having moved to the more luxurious Loudoun Road. But Springfield Road bears commemorating as the theatre in which she first came to see the emancipating potential of electricity for ordinary women and from where an extraordinary life and career had taken flight.

> We are coming to an Age when the spiritual and higher state of life will have freer development, and this is only possible when women are liberated from soul-destroying drudgery . . . I want her to have leisure to acquaint herself more profoundly with the topics of the day.
>
> Caroline Haslett[2]

33 WARWICK SQUARE, PIMLICO

Today, 33 Warwick Square is as imposing a building as when it was first built in 1859: a vast, red-brick mansion, heavily clad in ivy, with generous, black-framed sash windows designed specifically to maximise the light within. It was commissioned by a wealthy Scottish portrait artist named James Rannie Swinton and he meant for it to impress – with great sweeping staircases, a ballroom and a lavish glass-topped conservatory, this was the first house in London to have been built as a home, a studio and a gallery space in one. Hefty and commanding, like a burly Scot, architecturally

---

[2] The Caroline Haslett papers, Archives of the Institution of Electrical Engineers, London: specifically, pp 38–9: Margaret Partridge to Caroline Haslett, May 28 & 29 1925, Correspondence with M Partridge & Co., 1925–26, Women's Engineering Society Papers, Archives of the Institution of Electrical Engineers, London.

the house is unlike any other in the area and would have made a consider-
able impression on Swinton's wealthy clientele. It caught the attention too
of another unconventional Londoner, just as keen to impress the affluent; a
woman who in 1900 rented a large and airy one-room studio at number 33
from where she would change the face of modern dance.

Isadora Duncan
(1877–1927)
Isadora Duncan, the beautiful young American dancer who moved
into the studio at 33 Warwick Square in 1900, was by then already well
known among London society folk. With her languorous manner of
speech and penchant for loose, Grecian tunics, she was widely adored
by all who saw her dance. Dancing for London's elite had become a
lucrative affair and she could now comfortably afford the significant
rent due for the studio. Moving-in day, then, was momentous: financial security was a brand new phenomenon for Isadora.

Two years earlier, when she had first arrived in London from her
native USA, things had been very different. After a few weeks, Isadora
and two of her three siblings had found their meagre funds to have
dried up. They were accustomed enough to penury, having lived precariously in the States since their father was imprisoned for various
transgressions, most of which had to do with his desire to accumulate
wealth and simultaneous disregard for the conventions of business.
Their mother had earned what she could by teaching piano, and the
children began to teach dance to the self-conscious offspring of the
well-heeled, along the East Coast. Isadora dabbled too in a little theatre, joining a New York theatre company and touring joylessly in an
array of small parts. She soon tired of the life she had carved out for
herself and so, in 1898, boarded a cattle boat, bound for England.

Two years on and Isadora had constructed a new reality for herself
in London, one in which her love of dance but dislike of the restrictive conventions of classical ballet had finally found an outlet, dancing
in the parlours of London society's elite. She attracted attention as
much for her exotic, unfettered appearance as for the curious manner

in which she performed. For her, dance was about freedom, and that meant dancing without shoes, stockings, or corsets. Within two seasons in London, she had come to see once and for all that conventional theatre, classical ballet, or anything bound by the creation, invention or whim of others was not for her. Her art was something altogether more free-flowing and unencumbered, and in that respect, it was entirely new. The press took to calling it 'Free Dance'. By 1900, Isadora had found her medium, and with it, her audience.

London loved her. She mixed with artists and musicians and was adored by Charles Hallé, the son of the orchestral founder, who was instrumental in introducing her to the best connected individuals in London. She soaked up the Pre-Raphaelite paintings of Burne-Jones and Dante Gabriel Rossetti at the National Gallery, taking inspiration from them in her dance and so grew further and further from what she condemned as the 'sterile gymnastics' of ballet. At Warwick Square, for the first time, she had space in which to devise large-scale solo work, casting off elaborate sets and shrewdly opting for a plain, simply lit backdrop, with grey voile curtains and rose pink lighting, which threw focus on the form and shape of her body as she moved.

To those who knew her, she was as elusive and maddening as she was vivacious and fun. She constantly reinvented her past; her memoirs are riddled with inaccuracies and inconsistencies. She stayed nowhere for very long and late in 1900, set off for Paris. By 1907 she had a global following. During her career she performed extensively in Russia, dancing for Lenin and leaving a lasting impression on Russian choreographer Mikhail Fokhine, who subsequently drew heavily on Duncan's dance, devising naturalistic ballet for the first time.

Duncan suffered a succession of tragedies which led her increasingly to an alcohol dependency; not least among her heartbreak was the loss of her two young children, who drowned, ages three and five, in the Seine in Paris when the car they were travelling in was involved in an accident. And her own death in Nice at the age of fifty, strangled

56

by her billowing scarf while travelling in a open-top car, was as the-atrical as her life, prompting Jean Cocteau to write, 'Isadora's end is perfect'.[3]

The studio at Warwick Square was the space in which she had first been able to realise the extent of her ambition. Isadora Duncan was an uncontainable force and her legacy to the world of contemporary dance is immeasurable; moreover, she proved that a single woman, with the strength of her convictions, could throw off the confines of convention and change everything.

3 CHESTERFIELD STREET, MAYFAIR

In the middle decades of the nineteenth century, stately Chesterfield Street in Mayfair was a vibrant address at which to have lived. At number 4, the Prince of Wales was a regular visitor, seeking fashion advice from the city's favourite dandy, Beau Brummell. Lord Dudley, foreign secretary under Canning's premiership, had lived at number 1 until his death in 1833. British Whig politician and distinguished diplomat, Sir Robert Adair, lived at number 11 until his death in 1855. The revered Napoleonic Naval Admiral, Thomas Cochrane, Earl of Dundonald, known to Napoleon as 'The Sea Wolf', was also one of Chesterfield Street's distinguished resi-dents. But in the mid-1840s, the razor-sharp masculinity of the street was cut through by the arrival of a single woman at number 3. She lived alone, but could have enjoyed no anonymity, as in the years prior to her arrival, her name had been on the lips of every Londoner. The scandal she had endured would have lasting consequences for the institution of marriage under British law.

CAROLINE NORTON
(1808–77)

Caroline Norton was a woman out of her time: fiercely bright and an established novelist and poet, she hailed from the literary and politi-cally well-connected Sheridan family. When she and her two sisters came out into society in 1826 and 1827, they made such an impact

---

[3] Farfan, Penny, *Women, Modernism, and Performance* (Cambridge University Press, 2004).

that they were widely referred to as 'The Three Graces', securing invitations to all of the most sought-after events of the season. Their father had died during the girls' adolescence, leaving their mother with a meagre income; when Caroline entered society in 1827, she was genteel, gifted but broke. She saw marriage as her only sure route to financial security. Her sisters married well, gaining titles, children and relative contentment. Caroline's life, by contrast, would almost certainly have been a happier one had she braved the life of a single woman.

In her first season, Caroline was widely admired but received no offers of marriage, so when an old acquaintance, lawyer George Norton, proposed, after some deliberation she accepted. In fact, Norton had very little inherited wealth behind him, though he concealed this from Caroline and her mother, and though trained, he saw the professions as beneath him, instead trying unsuccessfully to make a name for himself in Parliament. Worse, on their honeymoon, Norton revealed his aggressive, controlling nature, throwing a heavy inkstand and his collection of law books at his young wife and later, kicking her heavily in the ribs after she disagreed with something he had said. His aggression kept pace with his increasingly lacklustre career and failing fortunes, until 1835, when her fourth pregnancy ended in miscarriage after a particularly brutal assault from Norton.

Caroline Norton left her husband at that point and fled to her mother and her story might have ended there, had she not subsequently been pushed by a vengeful Norton into seeing her struggle through to a remarkably courageous conclusion.

Under the terms of nineteenth-century laws on marriage, Norton was under no pressure to return to his wife any of her possessions. Land, property, furniture, ornaments, jewellery, even clothing were defined by law as the sole possession of the husband, regardless of whether they had first belonged to his wife prior to marriage. The law recognised no legal existence of a woman once she married: she had no place in court and no claim on any possession, not even her own children, who were regarded as the sole possession of their father from the moment of their birth. Norton, in spite of widespread condemnation from many of his peers, laid claim to his legal privileges in full.

He sought a divorce but would agree to no compromise on a sharing of property, giving his wife nothing. Not her clothing, not her furniture, nor a home to live in. And not her children either. When at length he capitulated, agreeing to a pitiful income and custody, she agreed, seeing it as her only option. As soon as he got word, he u-turned, changing his offer from custody to limited access to their children.

It was a common enough story: women had found themselves in this position before and had been powerless to fight it. But Norton underestimated his wife. She realised no amount of negotiation between them was going to change anything. Well-connected within Parliamentary circles, she knew first-hand how parliamentary process worked and had taken an active part in political lobbying ahead of the 1832 Reform Act. If she wanted justice, and custody of her children, she realised she was going to have to take on not Norton, but the law itself.

Caroline Norton and the Sheridans were prominent Whigs and she had maintained close connections with senior members of the party throughout her marriage, despite her husband's Tory affiliations. One of her closest friendships was with Lord Melbourne, who had recently become Prime Minister. During their marriage, Norton had capitalised on his wife's intimacy with Melbourne, insisting she entreat him to secure her husband a position within the law after the disaster of his political career. But after their separation, having already denied his wife her home and her children, he now turned to the only thing of hers left in his power to destroy: her reputation.

Norton filed a Criminal Conversation suit against Lord Melbourne, accusing him of having had an extra-marital affair with Caroline in the parlour of their Westminster home. Private correspondence between them reveals a clear affection, and Melbourne would later provide for

Caroline in his will, but whether there had ever been an affair remains a subject of some dispute. In the event, Norton provided just two witnesses in support of his case, both domestic servants in his employ. Caroline would later recall the 'loathsome coarseness' of the scenes the servants falsely claimed to have witnessed; very hard for her to bear, widely distributed as they were in lurid pamphlets. The case was one of the biggest controversies of its day, discussed from society parlours to the back benches of Parliament. Norton did everything in his power to fan the flames that were engulfing the last vestiges of his wife's privacy, publishing prominent advertisements in the newspapers in which he aired their private business, and issuing detailed statements about his wife's alleged affair with Melbourne. These were days before the notion of a gutter press, but the scandal proved irresistible; one newspaper went so far as to implicate both of Caroline's respectably married sisters in the Melbourne 'conversation'.

In spite of everything, however, the evidence presented in court was thin and Norton's case was ultimately unsuccessful; moreover, it had earned him widespread condemnation for having embarked upon it in the first place. Though the nine-day trial almost brought down Melbourne's government, in the event his name was cleared and once the dust settled, his career was essentially unharmed.

For Caroline, however, the story was entirely different: she had been humiliated by her husband in court and in the newspapers who covered the story. A few devoted friends maintained their support and her uncle, Charles Brinsley Sheridan, offered her his Mayfair home. But many turned their backs, Melbourne removed his friendship to save his career and, worse by far, Caroline's children remained with their father.

Here again, Caroline's resilience reveals itself. From her uncle's home on Green Street in Mayfair, she began to study the laws pertaining to marriage, divorce and child custody. She issued a series of polemical pamphlets and began to lobby Members of Parliament. Thomas Talfourd, MP, presented her Infant Custody Bill to Parliament, pushing for non-adulterous wives to gain the right to seek custody of any children under the age of seven. The success of the Bill in 1839 was her first legal triumph, though Norton had anticipated his wife's success and ensured she could not benefit personally by taking their children to Scotland, where English law had no jurisdiction.

By the 1840s, Caroline inherited money following the death of her uncle Charles and set up home alone in 3 Chesterfield Street. She continued to publish her poetry and novels, moved in increasingly literary circles, counting Mary Shelley and William Makepeace Thackeray as friends. Norton continued to prevent her from seeing her children until the death of her youngest son from blood poisoning after a riding accident; in an uncharacteristic show of humanity, Norton sent for Caroline, but William died before she reached Scotland. After that, he permitted her regular access to their two surviving sons.

Her fight to get the rights of married women established by law was not over, however, and in 1855, she turned her attention to the Marriage and Divorce Bill that was under debate in Parliament. She published a powerful pamphlet, addressed directly to HM The Queen, detailing the worst excesses of the laws preventing women from legal possession of any kind within marriage; a wife couldn't even lay claim to her own salary, as Caroline Norton pointed out, whether she 'weed potatoes or keep a school'; it was legally her husband's to claim. She made public, too, the horrific circumstances of the abuse and assault she had endured during her marriage; her determination to throw into the spotlight the injustices of English law as doled out to its married women far surpassed any last desire to maintain her privacy or protect her reputation. 'It's a strange and crying shame,' she wrote, 'that the only despotic right an Englishman possesses is to wrong the mother of his children.'

London and the wider population of England listened. The Matrimonial Causes Act of 1857 included four clauses taken directly from Caroline Norton's pamphlets. In desperate personal circumstances, she held a mirror to the way in which the law perpetuated and enabled some of the worst abuses wreaked out by some men upon their wives and succeeded in making crucial and significant changes. For all that, she was no feminist, refusing to join the radical 'Ladies of Langham Place' who had actively supported her campaigns for both the Infant Custody Act and the Matrimonial Causes Act, and publicly stated her disapproval of the 'wild and ridiculous doctrine of equality'.

Feminist or not, Norton risked her privacy, dignity and reputation to bring to an end women's legal invisibility and to push through the first truly feminist changes to British law of modern times. She is commemorated, too, for bringing the awful reality of domestic violence out of the shadows and into a very public arena. In the early nineteenth century, spousal abuse had been seen as an inherently *lower-class* phenomenon, entirely unbecoming of a gentleman. The violent drunk, however, as Norton proved himself to be, knew no social boundaries and for the law to change, Caroline Norton saw no choice but to go public with the grim realities of her own marriage.

9 CARLOS PLACE, MAYFAIR

In 1891, Carlos Place and the adjoining Mount Row, part of the Duke of Westminster's estate in the heart of Mayfair, had undergone a recent facelift, carried out on the authority of the Duke in an attempt to attract a higher calibre of business and resident. The area had already drawn in names which are of some significance to us today: Josiah Wedgwood had opened his first London showroom in Carlos Place in 1766; the poet Shelley had eloped with Harriet Westbrook from nearby Mount Street in 1772 and a century later, in 1881, the irrepressible Oscar Wilde had briefly rented rooms at 9 Carlos Place before embarking on a journey of discovery and self-promotion to North America the following year. Whether the young, aristocratic married couple who moved into the entirety of 9 Carlos Place at some point after their marriage in June 1891 were aware of the notoriety of the previous occupant is unclear; certainly by 1895 Wilde was a cause célèbre thanks in no small part to his much-publicised libel case against the Marquis of Queensberry. But the young wife who now kept house at number 9 would soon prove herself to be no slave to tradition or convention.

LADY EVELYN ZAINAB COBBOLD
(1867–1963)

The daughter of the 7th Earl of Dunmore, Evelyn was neither demure, nor passive, nor inward-looking. Born in Edinburgh, during her childhood she had travelled extensively and had spent significant periods in Algiers and Cairo, raised by Muslim nannies and developing a habit of sneaking out from under the gaze of her governess to visit the mosque with the local children she had befriended. Her remarkable childhood had left her fully immersed in Arabic culture and enabled her to become a fluent Arabic speaker.

She first met Cobbold, descended from a wealthy family of brewers, in Cairo and the couple married there in April 1891. They travelled together extensively early in their marriage, and in between, she played the role expected of her: a leading socialite when in her Mayfair home and a talented gardener at their country home in Suffolk. On her Scottish estate, where she returned often, she threw herself into country pursuits and had a reputation as a crack shot and champion deerstalker. But the pull of the Middle East was in her bones and by the early twentieth century, she was spending an increasing amount of her time abroad, travelling without her husband, from whom she finally separated in 1922.

She published the first of her three travel journals in 1912, which were well-received by critics, but it was the pioneering journey she made at the age of sixty-five in 1933 which would see her catapulted onto the pages of every British newspaper.

By the time of her 1933 expedition, she had already declared herself Muslim, although there had been no moment of conversion. She had, instead, come to a steady realisation of the lifelong fact of her dedication to Islam, recalling how as a young woman she and some friends had been granted an audience with the Pope, who asked whether she was a Roman Catholic. Without hesitation, she had announced herself a devotee of Islam. 'What possessed me I don't pretend to know,' she said, reflecting only that from her earliest years she had been 'unconsciously a little Muslim at heart'.

Her audience with the Pope was a catalyst, a moment in which she said, 'A match was lit.'[4] What began at the Vatican cumulated with a pilgrimage to Mecca in 1933, an experience she detailed in her best-selling book, *Pilgrimage to Mecca*.

Cobbold's religious belief was a private, internalised conviction; she was one of many aristocratic Britons who were attracted to the mysticism of Sufi Islam during the turbulent early decades of the twentieth century. As far as her biographers are aware, she wasn't given to the more public aspects of Islamic practise: she wasn't known to devote herself to prayer throughout the day, nor to practice Ramadan, for instance. Nonetheless, her devotion and strength of conviction was without doubt entirely genuine. Upon her death in 1963, she was laid to rest at the top of a remote hill on her Glencarron estate, where the 200-strong deer population could run freely over her grave as she had desired. Further to her last wishes, she was interred facing Mecca, to the sound of a piper, while the Surah 'Light' from the Qur'an was recited in Arabic by an Imam from Woking, who had made the considerable journey to Inverness-shire by train.

Although regarded as something of an aristocratic eccentric, Evelyn Cobbold lived life according to the strength of her passions and convictions and is commemorated as the first British Muslim woman to have made the Hajj pilgrimage.

2 GRAFTON STREET, MAYFAIR

Grafton Street is a short stroll from Mayfair's Berkeley Square Gardens and in the mid-nineteenth century, it would have been a fascinating place to have visited. The census return of 1841 reads like a page from Hansard's Pocket Peerage. *At number 1 was Alexander Edward Murray, 6th Earl of Dunmore, and his wife, Lady Catherine Herbert, daughter of the Earl of Pembroke. Irish peer, Edward Hill-Trevor, 3rd Viscount Dungannon and Conservative MP for Durham, lived at number 3. His colleague and future Cabinet minister, William Jolliffe, 1st Baron Hilton, lived at number 6. Former Tory Chief Whip, William Holmes,*

---

4 Cobbold, Evelyn, *Pilgrimage to Mecca* (Arabian Publishing, 2009).

lived at number 10, where his close friends, the Duke of Wellington and Sir Robert Peel, were said to have been frequent house guests. Former Whig Chancellor, Lord Brougham, at number 4, was a champion of the Great Reform Act of 1832 and the abolition of slavery in 1833, though his reputation for arrogance made him unpopular even within his own party. He had become a household name in 1820 after he represented Queen Caroline during the hugely unpopular dissolution of her marriage from George IV, and six years later in 1826, had narrowly evaded a scandal by paying a hefty sum to keep his name out of the reveal-all, Memoirs of Harriette Wilson, a notorious courtesan. Another formidable character lived at number 7, Admiral Sir Fleetwood Pellew, whose early career promise had been scuppered by his notoriously harsh treatment of his crew, which had twice provoked mutiny.

Grafton Street, then, had colour and wealth. In 1841, many of its households listed a domestic staff in excess of a dozen people; these were grand, affluent homes. Among them, at number 2, lived 35-year-old Captain Edward Joseph Hill Jekyll of the Grenadier Guards and his young wife, Julia. Jekyll's family had an altogether softer reputation than many of his neighbours: his great-grandfather, a New England customs collector, was reputedly so courteous that he was known as the 'Darling of Fair Traders'; another eighteenth-century Jekyll ancestor had bequeathed part of his estate to help settle the national debt. Edward and Julia had had seven children in total, all of whom would enjoy success in a wide array of fields. Their fifth child, a daughter, was born at 2 Grafton Street in 1843, and would come to leave a significant and enduring legacy of her own.

GERTRUDE JEKYLL
(1843–1932)

There can be no doubt that Gertrude Jekyll, the fifth of seven children, was born into great privilege. Her first five years were spent at one of Mayfair's most exclusive addresses and if she had passed time staring out of the window into the street below, she would have been able to watch the comings and goings of some of the leading statesmen and aristocrats of the day. At the age of five, however, her family left the bustle of the capital in search of a greener, cleaner space in Surrey, surrounded by heathland and pine forests. Gertrude came to love the outdoors, and gained a reputation within her family as an untameable child, described affectionately by her father as 'a queer fish'.

As a young woman, Gertrude and her siblings kept impressive company, not least of which was the author Robert Louis Stevenson, a close friend of her brother Walter and author of the enduring novel, *The Strange Case of Dr Jekyll and Mr Hyde*. Stevenson almost certainly drew inspiration from the family for the name of his amiable, well-liked central character. Gertrude was especially drawn to those with an artistic bent, including sculptor and painter, George Frederick Watts, and artist, writer and textile designer, William Morris. The craftsmanship of the Arts and Crafts Movement drew Jekyll in, more so during her time studying at the Kensington School of Art, where she was a contemporary of Burne-Jones. She travelled widely during this period, across Europe, the Middle East and North Africa, drawing cultural references wherever she went.

Jekyll was a polymath, turning her hand to a wide variety of arts and crafts, from gilding and metalwork to watercolour, embroidery and photography; she was entirely at home in her father's workshop at their Surrey home, passing hours designing and constructing elaborate models. Her adherence to Arts and Crafts principles deepened, and steadily she began to channel her creativity into a new direction: garden design. She brought something entirely new to the field, a visionary combination of cutting-edge principles of planting, her knowledge of the colour wheel and her skill as a painter. In 1889, her vision came to the attention of a young architect named Edwin Lutyens, himself heavily influenced by the Arts and Crafts Movement.

Together, Lutyens and Jekyll designed and landscaped her own garden, on a piece of land she bought opposite her family home in Munstead, Surrey. The success of the garden lay in its painterly sweep of colour, almost impressionistic in its effect. She championed an entirely new form of garden design, conceiving of the herbaceous border for the first time and celebrating hardy perennials, choreographed in careful terracing. Her planting stood in huge contrast to the rigid and formulaic sweep of annuals favoured by those of conventional Victorian sensibilities, and in England's climate, it also made enormous sense. No longer did gardeners have to dig up that which they had planted only three months before, ready for the new season. For the first time, her gardens spotlighted the beauty of form and shape with sweeping colour blocking, sculptural evergreens and shady shrubberies.

During her lifetime, Jekyll designed more than four hundred gardens, her commissions exclusively drawn from elite British or North American society, many in collaboration with Lutyens and most resulting from her significant society connections.

Jekyll was never driven to design for the humble, the modest or the small-scale. With her sights fixed on the vast gardens of the wealthy, her success was as dependent on the privilege of her birth as on her innate artistry. But her vision was to set the tone for an entirely new era of garden design, one which would come to extend far beyond the privileged elite into which she was born, and which continues to influence British garden design to this day. And though every bit a Victorian, Gertrude Jekyll entirely rejected a life lived within the restrictive conventions of marriage and motherhood; single throughout her life, she devoted herself instead to the pursuit of her driving passion, garden design. For that, she is commemorated.

ROYAL ACADEMY OF ARTS, BURLINGTON GARDENS, MAYFAIR

Tucked into a side street on the corner of Savile Row, just off Piccadilly, Burlington Gardens today is dominated by the rear face of the Royal Academy of Arts; in the 1930s, the gallery space here was named the New Burlington Galleries. For twenty-four days in the summer of 1936, Burlington Gardens and the surrounding streets were descended upon by crowds so vast that police closed off either end of the street. What had

drawn Londoners' attention was the nation's first exhibition of interna-
tional surrealist artists, widely marketed by a British press who were either
wholly perplexed or entirely dismissive. The launch itself featured one of
the earliest pieces of British performance art, a performance often cited
as a curiosity that typified the mayhem of that summer. Thanks to the
surrealist lens of one little-mentioned French artist and photographer, the
performance piece would also become the most iconic photographic image
of the Surrealist Movement.

Claude Cahun
(1894–1954)

A woman wanders Trafalgar Square, dressed in a pure white bridal
gown with a tapered hemline and cinched-in waist. Her arms are
outstretched, supporting pigeons on satin evening gloves that
reach almost the length of her arms. Her expression is impossible
to see, shielded as it is by a veil of roses. Later, having stepped out
of the claggy heat of London in June 1936, the same figure wanders noiselessly through the throngs inside the New Burlington
Galleries, now clutching a false limb in one hand and an uncooked
pork chop in another, until the meat begins to reek in the heat and
is discarded.

This was the 'Surrealist Phantom', much talked of in pre-exhibi-
tion marketing, though few members of the press seemed at all sure
what to make of it. 'Pork Chop Mystery' was the headline under which
the *Nottingham Journal* covered the exhibition – for example, ending
the piece with the line, 'It is no good asking why'.

The woman behind the phantom's mask has been widely named
as Surrealist poet, Sheila Legge; the concept for the piece has been
attributed to one of the exhibition's organisers, surrealist poet David
Gascoyne, who had in turn taken inspiration from Salvador Dalí's
depictions of women with flower-masked faces. But the person behind
the camera goes largely unnamed in almost every source.

That photographer was Claude Cahun, a French artist and writer
whose work was one of the earliest ever to have challenged binary

definitions of gender, and whose prolific political writing looked to Marxism to tackle fascism and break out of Western political conventions. Her anonymity in connection to 'the 'Surrealist Phantom' was in keeping with the manner in which she lived her life: her vast and remarkable body of photographic work was only released in the years after her death by her life partner and step-sister, Marcel Moore.

Her early years, lived under her birth name, Lucy Renee Mathilde Schwob, had been characterised by hardship. Though she hailed from a literary family of some repute in France, Schwob had suffered anti-Semitic attacks as a schoolgirl, in large part because of the Dreyfus Affair, a *cause célèbre* in which a Jewish captain in the French Army was falsely accused of passing intelligence to the Germans during the Franco-Prussian war, and sentenced to life imprisonment. The affair had divided Paris and though still only a child, Lucy Schwob had experienced its malicious fall-out first-hand.

Her childhood was marred, too, by the failing mental health of her mother, who was incarcerated in a Parisian lunatic asylum. By early adulthood, Schwob began to address her own malaise by distancing herself from her childhood identity, renaming herself first, Daniel Douglas and later, the gender neutral, Claude Cahun. At the age of seventeen, she had fallen in love with a childhood friend, now working as a graphic artist named Suzanne Malherbe, who went by the name of Marcel Moore. (The two would later become step-sisters when Malherbe's mother married Cahun's father.) Cahun began to describe herself as 'neuter' rather than strictly male or female, writing, 'Shuffle the cards. Masculine? Feminine? It depends on the situation.'

She began to write extensively, initially for the stage, her monologues tackling issues surrounding femininity and gender in works such as *Heroines* (1925). By the early 1930s, Cahun had become associated with a group of revolutionary artists who, led by André Breton, began to embrace surrealist principles. By 1935, as fascism gained pace across Europe, Cahun had founded the anti-fascist movement, *Contre Attaque.*

Two years before the outbreak of the Second World War, Cahun and Moore moved to settle permanently on the island of Jersey, where locals were bemused by the way in which the eccentric French sisters went about daily life conspicuously free from all the usual social conventions. They bathed nude at sunset, walked blindfolded, led only by a cat on a leash, and appeared in public in costumes which often paid no heed to the social or gender norms of dress.

In June 1940 Nazi forces occupied the island: Cahun, a middle-aged lesbian, gender-neutral Jew, living openly in a same-sex relationship in the face of occupying fascist forces; a true encounter of surrealism and real life. Locals kept occupying forces from discovering the sisters were Jewish; the sisters kept hidden, too, that Moore spoke and wrote fluent German. Together, they embarked upon a remarkable resistance movement, creating the persona of 'Der Soldat ohne Namen' ('The soldier with no name'), in whose name they created leaflets, powerfully written so as to undermine the self-esteem of German soldiers and incite them to mutiny. They dropped their leaflets under the doors of German Army billets, tucked them under the windscreen wipers of German military vehicles, or rolled them up inside cigarette cases distributed widely across the island. Their campaign was so extensive that when German forces finally caught up with them, they were at first dismissive that two ageing middle-aged sisters represented the entire extent of the Jersey resistance movement behind 'Der Soldat ohne Namen'. In 1944, the women were imprisoned and sentenced to death, but the sentence was commuted and they were eventually released when war ended.

Throughout her life, Cahun's photographic collection shows a fascination with the idea of 'self': she constantly explores and reinvents herself, shaking off one identity no sooner she has picked it up. Her self-portraits are staged and theatrical, embracing key surrealist principles. But though she would express in her writing a desire to belong, to affiliate to a group or a movement, her conviction in the importance of an unfettered fluid sense of self, rather than a fixed, defined identity, prevented her from getting anywhere closer than the sidelines of the leading surrealist players.

In 1936 her presence at London's groundbreaking surrealist festival was a pivotal one, and the photographic legacy she left behind that summer was both enduring and iconic. But for all that, she kept herself simultaneously anonymous, marginal and deliberately sidelined. For Cahun, art was a way of life rather than a means by which she wanted to make herself known: only one of her photographs was published in her name during her lifetime. Consequently, her artistry, her photography, her writing and her views on politics, identity and gender which unpinned everything she did in life were hidden, unknown to all but a very few, until they were uncovered and celebrated for the first time in the mid-1980s.

Breton hailed Cahun as 'one of the most curious spirits of our time'.[5] Later, David Bowie would be drawn in by that same curious spirit and stage an exhibition of her work in 2007, describing it as 'really quite mad, in the nicest way'.[6] Bowie emphasised the impossibility of defining Cahun, not even through a twenty-first century lens, and hailed her critical role in the early origins of the Surrealist Movement, for which she was never fully credited.

Anonymity was exactly how Cahun wanted it: for her, celebrity was unthinkable. Those who choreographed the London exhibition of 1936 were masters at self-promotion but for Cahun, art and real life were inextricably intertwined and lived largely in those shadows thrown by the likes of Breton and Dalí.

Without Cahun's influence, surrealism would arguably have been a predominantly male movement, with little exploration of the way in which gender could be depicted. Cahun challenged artists to see gender, sexuality, beauty and identity as something entirely fluid; her work was ahead of its time and, to the modern eye, seems all the more remarkable for the fact she never intended it to have an audience. Her art was entirely personal and yet posthumously she has left a legacy that packs a strong punch and continues to bear influence to this day.

---

[5] Shaw, Jennifer L., *Reading Claude Cahun's Disavowals* (Routledge, 2017).

[6] *Tonight's High Line – David Bowie Recommends*, David Bowie Official Blog, www.davidbowie.com, 18 May 2007.

Time hasn't recorded where Cahun stayed in London in the summer of 1936; certainly, she made the crossing with the Bretons and it seems likely she would have spent the summer with them, perhaps in a Mayfair hotel. But while the nation's press focused on the rose-veiled Phantom that moved ostentatiously through the crowds on Burlington Gardens on the opening day of the exhibition, they entirely overlooked the quiet Frenchwoman, clutching a camera on the periphery of the theatre at play around her. While the Bretons made a stir in their emerald green glitz (hair, eyelashes, nails, suit, shoes . . .), Dalí near-suffocated, delivering his lecture in an airtight diving bell, and Dylan Thomas passed around teacups of boiled rope, asking po-facedly, 'Weak or strong?', the real phantom of surrealism moved unnoticed.

For her remarkable legacy, Claude Cahun is remembered.

ABERCONWAY HOUSE, 38 SOUTH STREET, MAYFAIR

ANNE MCLAREN
(1927–2007)

Anne McLaren was born into landed gentry, her father, Henry McLaren, 2nd Baron Aberconway. She was raised in Mayfair until 1939, when the family moved to their seat, Bodnant House in North Wales, at the outbreak of war. McLaren studied zoology and had a distinguished scientific career, working at University College, London, the Royal Veterinary College and later, at the Institute of Animal Genetics in Edinburgh. She was made a fellow of the Royal Society in 1975 and was appointed to sit on the committee which would later contribute to the Warnock Report in 1978, the findings of a parliamentary committee which advocated the inclusion of children with Special Educational Needs within mainstream schools for the first time. Her pioneering work on fertility in animals enabled the medical advances which led to the birth of the first test-tube baby, Louise Joy Brown, in 1978.

MONTAGU SQUARE, MARYLEBONE

LADY HESTER STANHOPE
(1776–1839)

Hester Stanhope was a tall, elegant woman, born into significant wealth with a reputation as a charming, if sometimes blunt, hostess. As a young woman, she lived at 10 Downing Street with her unmarried uncle, Prime Minister William Pitt the Younger, acting as his hostess and private secretary.

When Pitt died in January 1806, Stanhope was given a hefty annual pension by the British government and moved out of Downing Street and into Montagu Square before leaving London to travel abroad. For the rest of her life, she travelled extensively and gained a reputation for eccentricity, roaming the Syrian Desert with a caravan of twenty-two camels in search of the New Messiah, whom she had been assured by a fortune teller that she would marry. She eventually settled in southern Lebanon, where she shaved her head, accumulated huge debts and corresponded with Queen Victoria, referring to herself always as 'Queen Hester'. In 1815, Stanhope led the first archaeological expedition in Palestine of modern times, in Ashkelon, having happened upon a medieval Italian manuscript which told of Ottoman gold buried there. Her use of written sources to steer her dig was pioneering. Less impressive was what she did with the finds she unearthed. When instead of a haul of the Sultan's gold, she found a seven-foot, headless Greco-Roman marble statue, she ordered it to be broken into a thousand pieces and thrown into the sea.

96 JERMYN STREET, ST JAMES'S

FANNY CORNFORTH
(1835–1909)

Born Sarah Cox, Fanny Cornforth hailed from a humble working-class family in Brighton. As a young woman she moved to London, where in 1858, she met Pre-Raphaelite artist, Dante Gabriel Rossetti, who grew infatuated with her strong, striking features and flowing red hair. She became his mistress and muse, her face illuminated in a style that was a radical departure from the Victorian aesthetic.

Rossetti soon switched his affections to Jane Morris, wife of William Morris, and made Fanny his housekeeper rather than his lover, although there is evidence that a genuine affection remained between them for the rest of his life. In due course, Fanny moved out and married a Scottish-born innkeeper named John Schott, and together they ran the Rose Tavern, which stood at 96 Jermyn Street. She remained in close contact with Rossetti, returning often to nurse him through his failing health and briefly opening a Rossetti Gallery on Piccadilly, London, after his death, at which she and Schott sold off some of the paintings she had in her possession. Schott died in 1891 and seven years later, Cornforth returned to Sussex. Her story ended pitifully: with failing mental capacity, Fanny Cornforth spent the last years of her life at the West Sussex County Asylum in Chichester, finally being laid to rest in an unmarked pauper's grave.

LAUDERDALE MANSIONS, MAIDA VALE

COUNTESS EMILIE AUGUSTA LOUISE LIND AF HAGEBY (1878–1963) AND LEISA SCHARTAU (1876–1961)

Countess Emilie, known as Lizzy, came from a wealthy Swedish family. She moved to London in 1902, along with fellow Swede, Leisa Schartau, who had enrolled to study at the London School of Medicine for Women. During their studies, they lived with Margaret Damer Dawson (*see page 139*) at her first London home in Lauderdale Mansions.

At medical school, the two women were horrified by the extent and nature of experimentation on animals, a practice with which they went public in their hard-hitting 1903 title, *The Shambles of Science*. The book included a graphic description of the vivisection of a dog without anaesthesia, prompting a highly publicised court case, dubbed 'The Brown Dog Affair' (1903). Although the jury found against Lind and Schartau, the women maintained a sustained media campaign and as a result, a Royal Commission on vivisection was established in 1907, from which new, tighter legislation on animal welfare ensued. Anti-vivisectionists commissioned a statue commemorating the brown dog, which was erected in Battersea Park in 1906. It became the focus of heated attacks of vandalism by London medical students and required a twenty-four-hour police guard. A series of angry riots took place on the streets, with students clashing with anti-vivisectionists, police and trades unionists in what became known as the Brown Dog Riots. Finally, some three months later, in March 1907, Battersea Council took down the statue under the cover of darkness, with a protective police detail of 120 officers. A new brown dog statue was commissioned in its place in 1985 and stands in the park to this day.

82 BROOK STREET, NEAR HANOVER SQUARE, MAYFAIR

EDITH DURHAM
(1863–1944)
Edith Durham was born into a wealthy household in a grand Mayfair home with a resident butler, footman, cook and four housemaids. She was the oldest of nine children born to Arthur Edward Durham, a consulting surgeon. Edith trained at the Royal Academy of Art and, in her youth, enjoyed a brief career as a published illustrator. However, as with the lives of so many women through the ages, the death of her father saw Durham shelve her own aspirations in order to devote her life to the care of her ailing mother, as she was the only one of her siblings still living at home.

By the age of thirty-seven, Durham's mental health had become impacted by years spent as a carer, and on medical advice she went abroad in search of a different climate. Edith travelled to the southern Balkan coastline, an experience she found so entirely transformative the region was to become her life and passion for the next twenty years. She learned Serbian, published several books and immersed herself in the people and the culture. Her most controversial book was *The Sarajevo Crime*, published in 1925, which analysed the causes of the First World War. Eventually she became a widely regarded anthropological expert on King Zog and the mountain peoples of Albania, by whom she was treated as a national treasure and on whose behalf she fought to counter misconceptions and racial ignorance in the British press. She documented her travels across the region with a vast photographic collection, which is stored at the British Museum and the Royal Anthropological Institute in London.

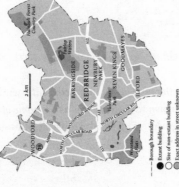

- - - - Borough boundary
● Extant building
○ Site of non-extant building
◉ Exact address in street unknown

CAMDEN

1. **Sarah Forbes Bonetta** (1843–80), 6 Cartwright Crescent, Bloomsbury WC1H 9EN.
2. **Helena Normanton** (1882–1957), 22 Mecklenburgh Square, Bloomsbury WC1N 2AD.
3. **Hilda Martindale** (1875–1952), 20 Mecklenburgh Square, Bloomsbury WC1N 2AD.
4. **Noor Inayat Khan** (1914–44), 4 Taviton Street, Bloomsbury WC1H 0BT.
5. **Pamela Lyndon Travers** (1899–1996), 49a Parkhill Road, Belsize Park NW3 2YD.
6. **Janet Lane-Clayton** (1877–1967), 2 Frognal Gardens, Frognal, Hampstead NW3 6XT.
7. **Beryl Ingham** (1901–60), 1 Albany Street, Regent's Park NW1.
8. **Adelaide Anne Procter** (1825–1864), 25 Bedford Square, Bloomsbury WC1B 3HW.
9. **Mary Somerville** (1780–1872), 12 Queen Square, Bloomsbury, WC1N.

ISLINGTON

10. **Mary Prince** (c. 1788–unknown), 60 Great Percy Street, Amwell Street, Clerkenwell WC1X 9ES.
11. **Dorothy Lawrence** (1896–1964), Marquess Road, Canonbury N1 2PX.

HACKNEY

12. **Angela Burdett-Coutts** (1814–1906), Holly Village, Highgate N6 6AA.
13. **Olive Christian Malvery** (1876–1914), Hoxton Hall, Hoxton Street, Hoxton N1 6SH.
14. **Jessica Tandy** (1909–94), 58a Geldeston Road, Cazenove E5 8SB.
15. **Helen Bamber** (1925–2014), 45 Amhurst Park, Stamford Hill, N16 5DL.
16. **Catherine Booth** (1829–90), 3 Gore Road, South Hackney, E9 7HW.
17. **Helen Taylor** (1831–1907), 4 Christopher Street, Shoreditch, EC1A 2BS.

HARINGEY

18. **Freda Lingstrom** (1893–1989), 105 Frobisher Road, Hornsey N8 0QU.

REDBRIDGE

19. **Joan Hughes** (1918–93), 'Eversley', Glengall Road, Woodford IG8 0DN.

CHAPTER SIX

Camden

6 CARTWRIGHT CRESCENT (FORMERLY BURTON CRESCENT), BLOOMSBURY

Bloomsbury's Burton Crescent at the turn of the twentieth century was a place of some notoriety. Already known to Trollope fans as the home of the lovelorn Johnny Eames in the 1864 novel, The Small House at Allington, *in 1878 the Crescent found itself the reluctant focus of significant media scrutiny. When one of its elderly residents was found murdered in her home, and an ensuing criminal trial proved inconclusive, relentless coverage by a salacious press meant Burton Crescent became synonymous with infamy. The association proved intolerable for its residents, who subsequently petitioned successfully for the street to be renamed 'Cartwright Crescent'. But in 1861, Burton Crescent was as yet a quiet and unremarkable address, home to an interesting and diverse mix of professionals, including several professors of music, a few physicians, one or two Church of England clergymen, numerous upstanding members of the London Jewish community and an expert on military pigeons. At number 6, amid this fittingly eclectic setting, lived one of Victorian Britain's most unusual women.*

SARAH FORBES BONETTA
(1843–80)

A little after noon one Saturday in August 1862, the London Fire Engine Establishment, as the Fire Brigade were officially still known, were alerted to a house fire at number 6, Burton Crescent. Owned by a Mr Moses, the only occupants of the house that day were his guests, newly-weds Captain James Davies and his young wife, Sarah Forbes Bonetta, who were a week into their marriage and honeymooning in Bloomsbury. The fire-fighters caught the fire early enough to contain it to a single room, no doubt to the relief of all concerned. Bizarrely, later that same evening, a second fire on the top floor went undiscovered long enough to take hold, so that before it could be contained, it had destroyed much of the top floor and the roof above. The majority of the young couple's wedding gifts were destroyed in the process, either by the fire itself or by subsequent water damage.

That Sarah Forbes Bonetta's married life could have begun with such drama must have felt entirely in step with the series of remarkable events which she had already endured over the course of her nineteen short years. Much of the first five years or so of Sarah's life were a mystery to her. She had been born a princess, a long way from Bloomsbury, that much she knew. And until the age of eight, her name had been Aina, daughter of the King of the Egbado people, a clan within the Yoruba tribe of south-western Nigeria. Aina was the name given to baby girls born with the umbilical cord around their necks: even the moment of her birth, then, had been eventful. At the age of five, she witnessed the sacking of her village and the decapitation of her parents at the hands of the Dahomeyan Army, who were sweeping the region on a slave hunt; she would never know what became of her siblings. As the firstborn of royal lineage, she was held captive at the court of the Dahomeyan King Ghezo. There, she remained for the next two or three years, enslaved and destined to be used as a ritual sacrifice upon the death of the King. But the arrival of a British naval captain named Frederick Forbes in 1850 was to alter the course of her life unrecognisably.

Forbes was an emissary of the British government, on a mission to persuade Ghezo to call a halt in his trade with South American and Portuguese slavers. Ghezo made him a gift of the child, 'From the King of the blacks to the Queen of the whites', a gift designed to embarrass Victoria and her anti-slavery government. Aware that if he were to refuse what he would later describe as an 'extraordinary present', the child would have faced a grim future, Forbes took her on, renamed her Sarah and returned with her to England on his ship, HMS *Bonetta*, which he combined with his name to give the child a surname.

Freed from African slavery she may have been, but the child's life would still not be her own. Robbed of her family, her people, her home, and now also her name, an audience with Queen Victoria at Windsor Castle would further alter the path her life was to take.

Forbes recalled in his diary that Sarah was a remarkably bright child: by the time she arrived on British soil, she was already fluent in English, self-taught during the crossing. In what must have been an overwhelmingly alien setting, she was able to recount her story to a rapt royal audience. Victoria was captivated and agreed to provide for her at Captain Forbes's Berkshire home, as a royal god-daughter.

Sarah was provided with a handsome annual allowance and lived within the Forbes family at their home in Berkshire. She was a regular visitor to the Palace, was schooled in royal etiquette and became a close companion of the Queen's daughter, Princess Alice. The Queen began to call her 'Sally' and her diaries and correspondence suggest she was inordinately fond of her.

The Queen's generosity towards the child was undoubtedly well-intended but its impact upon Sarah's life and liberty was significant. Royal privilege came at a cost. Sarah's movements were well documented in newspaper columns devoted to the comings and goings at court; she became a celebrity. When the British climate took its toll on Sarah's health in 1851, the Queen decided she should continue her education in Africa, at the Church Missionary School in Sierra Leone, where Sarah was reportedly deeply unhappy. Four years later, back in England, the untimely death of Captain Forbes came as another blow, and saw Sarah relocated to Kent, to reside with another family, hand-selected by the Queen.

And then, at eighteen, a proposal of marriage. Her suitor was a widower, thirty-one years old, himself born into slavery in Nigeria, before being liberated and taken into service with the Royal Navy. He had proved himself, climbing to the rank of captain and by the age of thirty-one, he was a wealthy merchant in his own right, employing around a hundred men.

Sarah's letters make it plain that she had no interest in marrying

Captain James Davies and she resisted. Victoria's responses make it plain she had no choice: to refuse what the Queen felt to be an eminently suitable husband would see an end to her royal patronage. Victoria relocated Sarah again, this time to the home of two elderly sisters in Brighton, whom she felt best-placed to see her received into society. It has been mooted by some that this was a strategic move on Victoria's part: certainly, Sarah loathed her new home, which she described as 'a desolate little pig sty', a taste, perhaps, of the level to which she would be reduced should she persist in refusing the Captain.

She didn't persist for long: the wedding came within a year. It was an extravagant event, with the dress gifted by the Queen and every detail covered in significant column inches across the country.

Whether the fires of the honeymoon were in any way a product of Sarah's reluctance about the union is impossible to know from this distance, but in any case later correspondence suggests that in time, she came to love her husband. They settled in Lagos, had three children and maintained their close links with the British Court.

Sarah Forbes Bonetta is remarkable for spotlighting the central role women of colour have long weaved, at every level, in the fabric of London life. She is remarkable for her resilience in the face of unimaginable suffering and upheaval; for her poise, her intelligence, her dignity, traits remarked upon by all who knew her. She is remarkable for her charisma, her capacity to captivate all who met her. She is remarkable, too, for challenging ordinary Britons to look at Empire in a new light. For the way in which the British press of the 1860s wrote about her with all the awe and reverence afforded any other member of the British aristocracy, while boasting in the next sentence of the contrast this represented to the lives of people of colour on the other side of the Atlantic, where almost four million enslaved people had been listed in the US census of 1860, and where the issue had driven a nation to Civil War in 1861. Against that backdrop, Sarah's celebrity, and her immersion within the British Royal Court was a matter of national pride, making her a worthy candidate for commemoration.

20 AND 22 MECKLENBURGH SQUARE, BLOOMSBURY

The houses lining the eastern edge of Mecklenburgh Square in Bloomsbury were designed to attract the best possible residents. At the turn of the eighteenth century, the governors of London's Foundling Hospital for unwanted infants commissioned the square to be built on land adjacent to the hospital site. The first phase of housing, on the south side of the square, had failed to impress. It has since been entirely destroyed in bombing raids during the Blitz, but when newly built, the south side had not attracted the calibre of occupants the hospital governors had hoped for. Consequently, when it came to the designs for the second phase, on the east side, the governors had their surveyor try harder. What resulted was a palace facade, a row glistening in white stucco, one section of which at least escaped the Luftwaffe in the 1940s and stands today, numbers 20 and 22 among them. And in 1919, at the end of the First World War, these would become home to two women, each driven to fight for equality for women within the workplace.

One, a feminist, academic and pacifist, who had fought hard for women's suffrage, campaigned for women's equal rights within marriage and employment, and had now set her sights on something even more ambitious. The other, fighting for women's workplace rights, battling against gender discriminatory employment practices and proving by her word, deed and prowess that women were every bit as capable as their male colleagues of taking senior office. At last, the houses were no longer remarkable simply because of their elaborate frontage, but because of those who lived within.

HELENA NORMANTON
(1882–1957)

Helena Normanton had a difficult start in life. Born in Stratford, East London, her father, a piano maker, was found dead in a railway tunnel when Helena was just four years old. His neck had been broken in a brutal assault. Helena was subsequently raised in Brighton by her mother and witnessed first-hand how hard it could be for a woman to support her family and be taken seriously in a male-dominated world. When she lost her mother as a teenager, Helena determined to work hard to ensure she would never be financially reliant on anyone but herself. In that context, signing the lease on her own home at number 22, Mecklenburgh Square in 1919 saw a major life-goal achieved; but by then, her ambition and achievements extended far beyond financial security.

Normanton was a woman of conviction and her life stands testament to her determination to stand by those convictions no matter what cost. She began her professional career as a teacher but grew increasingly uncomfortable with a curriculum which preached Imperialism when everything she read about India, for instance, left her a passionate supporter of self-determination. Unable to marry up the conflict between the two positions, she left the profession.

As a young woman, Normanton was an active member of the militant women's suffrage movement, but in 1907, she joined forces with a seventy-strong group of women who broke free from the Women's Social and Political Union to establish the non-violent Women's Freedom League. She wrote extensively on women's issues, including her 1914 pamphlet, *Sex Differentiation in Salary*, which argued for equal pay in return for equal work. Normanton saw gender inequality embedded within the fabric of society and she set herself against it from an early age. In her 1932 publication, *Everyday Law for Women*, she recalled an uneasy encounter in a solicitor's office when she was twelve years old. She described how the solicitor failed to make himself understood, and how she then recoiled at his condescension when her mother asked that he explain himself more simply. The experience left Normanton determined to pursue two more goals: to ensure that women had access to the law, and to become a lawyer herself.

In this respect, Helena Normanton was a true pioneer. She had studied History, gaining a First class honours degree while working as a teacher. In 1918, she applied to become a student at the Middle Temple. As she had anticipated, she was refused on the grounds of her gender, so she petitioned the House of Lords. The following year, she made a second application to the Bar, within hours of the Sex Disqualification (Removal) Act being passed, and this time she was accepted.

In 1921, Normanton married Gavin Bowman Watson Clark while

studying at the Bar, but fought to retain her maiden name – and therefore her identity – when she qualified: an unprecedented and therefore controversial position to have taken. She had long campaigned for married women to be given the right within law to maintain property, money and income separately from their husbands and in this respect, too, lived her life according to her convictions. In 1924, she became the first married woman in the UK to hold a passport in her maiden name, establishing the right for others to follow suit.

In 1922, she became the second woman in the UK to be called to the Bar and the first ever to practise. As the only woman in practice, naturally her gender remained a barrier, made more challenging because she had neither an Oxbridge education nor a well-connected family on which to build a network of support within the profession. Often pilloried in the press, not least because of her past history as a militant suffragist, she found many solicitors hesitant to work with her and continued to receive malicious mail for many years, all objecting to her presence in the profession. As a result, she struggled to make a living from practice and took in lodgers at Mecklenburgh Square, as her mother had done before her in Brighton, to make ends meet.

Her legal career was nonetheless remarkable, breaking down barrier after barrier in her plight for gender equality. She was the first woman to represent clients in the High Court and at the Old Bailey; the first to conduct a trial in America; the first to obtain a divorce for her client; the first to lead the prosecution on a murder case, and one of two women who were the first to be made King's Counsel in 1949. She weathered the storm and in so doing, paved the way for women to practise.

The child raised by a single parent, orphaned in her teens, from a family with no history of a university education, had battled disadvantage and broken barriers at every stage of her career. Not only was the home she leased on Mecklenburgh Square testament to her determination to secure her own livelihood, separate and distinct from her spouse, but it was also the setting in which, against all odds, she broke the gender barrier within legal practice. Helena Normanton's pioneering and important career as a feminist and a lawyer has gone largely unnoticed in our history books; recognition is long overdue.

HILDA MARTINDALE
(1875–1952)

It seems highly probable that Hilda Martindale, who also moved into Mecklenburgh Square in 1919, at number 20, had long known her neighbour, Helena Normanton (*see page 83*). Like Normanton, Martindale had also been raised in Brighton by a strong, single mother, widowed during her pregnancy with Hilda. Martindale's mother, Louisa Martindale, had been a leading figure within the Congregationalist Free Church and an active figure within the local community of Brighton, involved with the Women's Co-operative Movement and founding the Women's Liberal Association.

Inspired by the feminist writing of Mary Wollstonecraft, Louisa Martindale came to see that her two daughters ought to have the same rights within education and employment as men. She had worked closely with her brother, James Spicer, Member of Parliament for Monmouth and later for Hackney, fighting for women's rights to gain employment within local councils. She had been ceaseless in her efforts to further the lot of British women, and it is of little surprise that both her daughters grew to be true pioneers. Her elder daughter, also named Louisa, was one of the early cohort of women to study medicine and went on to become the country's first female GP. Hilda's career was every bit as remarkable, but took an altogether different route.

After completing her studies in hygiene at Royal Holloway and Bedford Colleges in 1898, Hilda Martindale had for a time worked for Dr Barnado's, inspecting the homes in which orphaned children were fostered out. But in 1901, she took a new direction, one in which she admitted to having no prior expertise. She joined the Home Office, becoming one of the first women in the country to be employed as a factory inspector. Women had only been permitted to gain employment within the Civil Service for the first time in 1869 and by the turn of the century, their role was still limited. A commission carried out within the Service in 1874 concluded that 'women are well qualified for clerical work of a less important character and are satisfied with a lower rate of pay than is expected by men similarly employed'. However, almost twenty years later in 1892, unease about the working conditions of women in factories prompted the Home Secretary, Herbert Henry Asquith, to appoint the first two female factory inspectors.

Hilda therefore joined a small women's division of the Factories Inspectorate that was barely a decade old. She and her colleagues were sent across Britain and Ireland, to factories that had often already been inspected by men. Unsurprisingly, the women were met with widespread resentment and any critical reports they sent back about the working or sanitary conditions they found were regarded by many as 'spying'. It was an uneasy role to be in.

Nonetheless, Hilda Martindale proved dedicated to her work, publishing a report on the incidence of lead poisoning among brick factory workers in Ireland that was to prove a catalyst for investigation into the working conditions for women in Irish factories. Martindale was made senior lady inspector in 1914, one of the first women to have risen to a senior position within the Civil Service. With the appointment coming at the outset of the First World War, her role was to prove critical in organising the appointment of women to fill industrial posts left vacant by men on the Front; with the advent of peace, Martindale's service was rewarded with an OBE.

She continued to rise through the ranks of the Civil Service, becoming deputy chief inspector of factories in 1925, a remarkable success for an era in which most forms of employment were still largely segregated by gender and within an organisation which famously looked with scepticism at the promotion of women above a certain rank. The restrictions on career progression for women was an issue with which Martindale became increasingly preoccupied. Not only would her salary have been at most 60 per cent of that of her male counterparts, the future of her career hinged on one critical life decision: her marital status. In the 1920s, the Civil Service, in common with the teaching profession and many other organisations, operated a strict marriage bar. Once a woman married, it was widely perceived that she could not devote herself to two roles, that of wife and employee. Martindale became a member of the Whitley Council Committee at which she was a fervent champion of equal pay for women and pushed hard for an end to the marriage bar. She argued that the decision as to whether a woman's marriage could happily co-exist with her job should be a matter strictly for individual women to decide. She fought too for the right of women to be posted overseas within the Foreign Office, something which met with much resistance even after the Sex Disqualification (Removal) Act of 1919, which had upheld the right for the Civil Service to reserve overseas postings for men only. Martindale lobbied hard to get this ruling overturned, arguing that women had long proved their professionalism when working overseas as doctors, teachers or nurses.

In the event, the marriage bar remained in place within the Civil Service until 1946, and even then, the problem persisted for two or three decades more, with women routinely employed on temporary contracts which could be terminated upon their marriage. Without doubt, however, Martindale's remarkable career laid the foundations for successive generations of women to rise beyond clerical ranks and prove their worth at every level. Indeed, Martindale's uncle, her mother's brother, James Spicer, was great-grandfather to Labour MP, Harriet Harman. For Louisa and Hilda Martindale, both champions of women's rights within Parliament and the workplace, there is perhaps no more fitting a legacy than a female descendant sitting within the House of Commons.

4 *TAVITON STREET, BLOOMSBURY*

Taviton Street in the heart of Bloomsbury's Bedford Estate is now largely given over to University College London, but for the most part of the nineteenth century, a gate at the eastern end of the street was one of five dotted around the perimeter of the estate, designed to stop Londoners using the area as a thoroughfare. By 1890 it had become clear that all efforts at privacy were in vain and the gates were removed. The Duke of Bedford, who owned the land, had gone to some lengths to maintain a good standard of living for his tenants in an effort to attract a desirable sort; as early as the 1850s he constructed new sewers and had water closets installed inside all the properties on the estate.

As the nineteenth century came to a close, Taviton Street was attracting an unlikely mix of actors and clergymen, and in 1914, a new family arrived on the street and moved into number 4. Fresh from Moscow, they were of exotic descent and their newborn baby girl, born in a monastery a mile from the Kremlin, would prove herself one of London's most courageous daughters.

NOOR INAYAT KHAN
(1914–44)
Noor Inayat Khan was a well-travelled, talented writer and musician of royal stock, born in Russia of Indian descent and praised widely by those who knew her for her self-effacing spirit. She was a Sufi Muslim who sacrificed her pacifist principles and ultimately also her life to fight fascism as a spy within the British Special Operations Executive (SOE) during the Second World War.

Noor's royal heritage came through her father's line. Inayat Khan was a descendant of the revered eighteenth-century ruler of Mysore, Tipu Sultan, and hailed from a long line of poets, mystics and musicians. Inayat himself was a classically trained musician who had had a successful career performing across Europe and North America, but by 1914 he had also come to be recognised as the founder of Sufism in the West, teaching a mystical branch of Islam he named 'Universal Sufism'. During the years of the First World War and in its immediate aftermath, lectures on Islamic mysticism given by Khan were listed in regional newspapers the length and breadth of the UK and his following began to grow.

In common with her elder brothers, Noor proved a talented scholar and a gifted musician. The family left London in the 1920s and relocated to Paris, where she trained at the Sorbonne and made a career for herself as a children's writer. But when France was invaded by Nazi forces, Noor felt her family's pacifist convictions challenged by the impact of an invading aggressor. The family fled Paris and returned to London; as soon as they arrived, Noor signed up with the Women's Auxiliary Air Force.

Noor excelled throughout her training and was posted to Bomber Command, but her prowess and fluency in French brought her to the attention of Churchill's self-described 'Ministry for Ungentlemanly Warfare', a newly formed secret service called the Special Operations Executive. She was interviewed for the SOE in a shabby hotel off Trafalgar Square and the offer presented to her was not for the faint-hearted. To work behind enemy lines would leave SOE operatives entirely unprotected: capture would mean inevitable torture and probable death. Noor didn't hesitate and the strength of her conviction impressed itself on her interviewer, Captain Selwyn Jepson, enough for him to forgo the usual second and third interviews. Her letter of acceptance outlined her concern at leaving behind her family and her fiancé, but in it she described these family ties as 'petty' in the face of so grave a threat to freedom as Nazism. Whether Noor was aware at this stage that a covert radio operator on French soil had a life expectancy of just six weeks is unclear.

The training was tough and her instructors credited her for her diligent perseverance with skills they could see didn't come easy to her: weapons and sabotage training could not have come instinctively to the woman whose childhood had been characterised by meditation, prayer and a tendency towards dreamy romanticism. Colleagues began to voice concerns that this dreaminess, coupled with her exotic good looks and inherent inability to lie, made her far too conspicuous for life as a secret agent.

In spite of the divided opinions about her suitability, in June 1943 Noor Inayat Khan became the first woman dropped by Allied forces behind enemy lines as a covert wireless operator. The wireless radio filled a heavy suitcase, and before she could broadcast messages, she needed to extend a seventy-foot-long aerial. It was perilous work.

Just five days after Noor began sending intelligence back to England, the resistance network within which she was operating was infiltrated by the Gestapo and arrests were made. This left Noor the sole Allied wireless operator on French soil, the last remaining link with London; the SOE promised to get her out as a matter of urgency but she declined. The Gestapo knew of her existence, though they had only her code name 'Madeleine', and now threw all their resources into tracking her down. Noor must have known at this point that her days were numbered, but telling London that her presence was more important than ever, she continued broadcasting, extending her reach to act for other British agencies. For three months, she drew upon everything she had learned in her training to keep clear of the Gestapo and was able to co-ordinate the delivery of vital funds and equipment to the resistance and secure the safe passage home of thirty Allied airmen.

Just as London sent word that her replacement was on her way over to France, Noor's whereabouts were betrayed by a Frenchwoman and she was captured. She was held at Gestapo headquarters in Paris but refused to pass on any information; despite lengthy interrogations, the Gestapo were unable to make a single additional arrest. Several times Noor was caught trying to escape and subsequently refused to sign a promise that she would desist from any further escape efforts; it was her duty, she told her captors, to continue to try. That same incapacity to lie that had first been flagged by her SOE trainers back in England would finally prove her undoing. Branded a significant risk, she became the first captured SOE operative to be sent to Germany, where she was beaten and interrogated for a further ten months, all the while refusing to reveal anything of damage to the Allied war effort. Finally, in September 1944, she was transferred to the concentration camp at Dachau, along with two other SOE operatives. On arrival, she was beaten through the night and executed at dawn.

Posthumously, Noor's extraordinary courage was rewarded with a

Croix de Guerre in France and her former family home in suburban Paris is honoured annually on Bastille Day by a military band. Noor Inayat Khan was the first Muslim woman of the Second World War to be awarded the George Cross in Britain, the highest civilian bravery award, the citation for which praises her for displaying 'the most conspicuous courage, both moral and physical over a period of more than 12 months'.

London was graced with Noor's presence at 4 Taviton Street during the years of the First World War, when she spent her days in dreamy pursuits in Gordon Square Gardens, and again briefly in 1942, during her SOE training. For her courage, her sacrifice and for the strength of convictions, she is remembered.

43A PARKHILL ROAD, BELSIZE PARK

From the 1920s until the Second World War, Parkhill Road in Belsize Park was home to a remarkable number of artists. Barbara Hepworth, John Skeaping and Ben Nicholson all took up residence on the street. The outbreak of the Second World War saw Hepworth escape London for the safety of Cornwall, and Henry Moore and his wife, Idina, move into their studios. Hepworth had made a wise move, as it turned out: her former studios took a direct hit in 1940, destroying all the work Moore was housing there. With Ben Nicholson's encouragement, the Dutch artist, Piet Mondrian, moved into number 60 in 1938. It was quite a neighbourhood and among these illustrious names, in the late 1920s, a young Australian woman took a flat at number 43a, with her close friend, Madge. Although not an artist, she would immerse herself in London life, mix with some of the leading figures of the time and leave a literary legacy that has endured to this day.

PAMELA LYNDON TRAVERS
(1899–1996)

Pamela Lyndon Travers's start in life was far from idyllic. Born in Australia, her parents' marriage was strained: her father, a banker, demoted from manager to clerk because of the destructive impact of his battle with alcoholism; her mother, the sister of the Australian premier, never recovered from her sense of having married beneath her. After her father died when she was still only seven years old, Pamela grew close to her great-aunt Ellie, a force of nature whom Travers later recalled was never without a carpet bag.

In 1924, Travers moved to London and threw herself into everything the capital had to offer. She soon found a market for her poetry and journalism, particularly with the *Irish Statesman*, through which she befriended some of the leading Irish writers of the age, including A. E. Russell, W. B. Yeats and George Bernard Shaw, characters she said, 'all cheerfully licked me into shape'.

Russell introduced Travers to a young woman named Madge Burnand, with whom she formed a close friendship. By the 1930s, Travers and Burnand were living together at 43a Parkhill Road. Later, they also took a cottage together in rural Sussex, from where in 1933 Travers began to write the first of a series of novels about the trials and tribulations of a London family struggling to cope through the Depression. This was *Mary Poppins*, a woman altogether more steeped in the world of the occult and mysticism than Disney would later reveal. A woman who rescued the children in her care, set them on a path to self-discovery but who nonetheless was possessed of dark powers and brought as much threat as she did hope. The character had lodged herself in the recesses of Travers's mind since the miserable childhood she had long since reinvented. And under the influence of the theosophy, spiritualism and mysticism she had first encountered with Russell in Dublin, Poppins emerged a mythical creature whom Travers would later compare to the Hindu Mother Goddess, Kali.

Travers famously resisted the adaptation of her great *oeuvre* by Disney until the 1960s, and remained resistant to much of what Disney and his team wanted to do with the movie; she shed tears throughout the premiere. But her literary prowess was nonetheless remarkable: Sylvia Plath, for one, held *Poppins* in high regard.

During the Second World War, Travers spent two summers working in the US for the Office of War Information. She was sent by a friend of hers to live on the Navajo reservations as a cure for homesickness. There, she donned the wide Spanish-style skirts and little velvet jackets worn by the Navajo women and became fascinated with their culture, myths and traditions. She spent time too with the Hopi people and the Pueblo people. Her love of myth remained a lifelong passion and later she spent time in Japan studying Zen mysticism.

She once told *The Paris Review* that she had not consciously created Poppins: 'I cannot summon up inspiration. I myself am summoned.' Certainly, her love for the mysterious woman who blew in with the wind was lifelong: journalists interviewing her at the age of ninety-five found her re-reading the *Mary Poppins* series, and when asked if she felt proud, she replied simply, 'I really got to know her.'

By the end of the war, Travers left Belsize Park and Hampstead and took a two-storey flat in a Georgian terrace at 50 Smith Street in Chelsea. But the Hampstead she knew is embedded within her novels: the eccentric Admiral Boone, who periodically shakes up the neighbourhood by firing cannons from his rooftop, is based on Admiral's House, Admiral Walk, Hampstead Grove, built by an eccentric retired naval officer during the reign of George III. The lieutenant had a main deck and a quarter deck, along with a captain's cabin, constructed on the roof of the house from where he was said to have fired a cannon to mark the King's birthday.

Travers spent the latter decades of her life on a pretty Chelsea street named Shawfield Street, at number 29. Of all the white terraced houses on the street, number 29 was the only one with a vibrant pink front door, in honour of number 17, Cherry Tree Lane. She remains one of the greatest story-tellers in the English language and for that, London remembers her.

2 FROGNAL GARDENS, FROGNAL, HAMPSTEAD

At the time of the census in 1901, the grand pairs of houses lining Frognal Gardens were only ten years old. They had been built in the 1890s along an L-shaped road laid down within the grounds of the old Frognal Mansion. Their warm terracotta-coloured brick, Flemish-style roof lines, corner towers with oriel windows and great sweep of steps leading from the pave-ment to the first-floor entrance were classic Queen Anne revival and not to everyone's taste. Some contemporary commentators regarded them as 'coarse', and in her 1900 book, Sweet Hampstead, *local author Caroline White criticised the 'scarlet-faced mansions' for having destroyed the rural idyll for which Frognal had been renowned in the 1880s. Nonetheless, the homes attracted a crop of professional middle classes; heading every house-hold were architects, solicitors, civil servants or men who had inherited sufficient wealth to describe themselves as 'of independent means'.*

Noticeably, in 1901, the only working women listed on the street were domestic staff, employed in some number in each home. The family at number 2 was no exception: Joseph Lane-Claypon was the director of a bank and a Justice of the Peace; his wife kept home, with the help of a resident footman, a cook and two domestic servants. The second of their four children, however, would prove to be every bit the twentieth-century woman. Listed in 1901 as a 24-year-old medical student, her career would prove to be one of the most pioneering of the age and still has impact today.

JANET LANE-CLAYPON
(1877–1967)

When the Medical Research Council issued its first annual report in 1915, Janet Lane-Claypon was the only female named researcher among a sea of men. She had first taken up her studies at the London School of Medicine for Women in 1898, little more than two decades after it had first been established by Elizabeth Garrett Anderson, Sophia Bex-Jake and Elizabeth and Emily Blackwell. By 1910, Lane-Claypon would have more than proved her worth as a doctor, with an impressive string of qualifications and fellowships to her name, including a First class honours degree, an MD and a doctorate in phys-iology. Her appearance in the MRC's report is a measure of quite how exceptional a practitioner a woman had to prove herself in order to achieve the same recognition as her male colleagues.

Lane-Claypon began her career as a research scientist, specialising in the field of epidemiology, looking at patterns and causes of disease.

The work for which she was mentioned by the MRC in 1915 was in fact a result of the first research grant the Council had ever awarded to a woman. In carrying out her research, Lane-Claypon had pioneered the use of cohort studies, specifically looking at the impact of breast-feeding over bottle feeding in a study of over five hundred women. She took into consideration other potentially confounding features of the women within each cohort, including socio-economic factors, for example. Not only were Lane-Claypon's findings to form the corner-stone of modern understanding about the benefits of breast milk, but her meticulous methodology and, in particular, the central principle of the cohort study would also prove pioneering, entirely transforming the science of epidemiology.

By 1923, Lane-Claypon had moved into public health, carrying out extensive research into breast cancer on behalf of Neville Chamberlain at the Ministry of Health. She discovered a clear correlation between incidence of breast cancer and a number of other factors, including the number of children a woman had, the age at which she had first given birth, and the age at which she had first begun to breastfeed. Modern research into breast cancer has upheld all of Lane-Claypon's key findings, but as with her earlier research into breast milk, the find-ings themselves were only part of her legacy.

In order to gather and assimilate the quantity of data she had needed, Lane-Claypon had undertaken the first ever case control study, gathering data from six hospitals over a number of years from women of very similar backgrounds and circumstances, some of whom had the disease, some of whom didn't, in order to analyse those aspects of lifestyle which might point to a possible cause.

Lane-Claypon's rigorous dedication to pioneering research tech-niques enabled a significant advance in the understanding of the benefits of breastfeeding and in the causes of breast cancer. A further study, which she published at the Ministry of Health in 1926, looked at comparative survival rates of breast cancer patients who had received different forms of treatment, at different stages of the disease. It was the first end-study in the field of epidemiology.

Lane-Claypon's legacy is irrefutable; it seems unthinkable to a modern eye, therefore, that a woman called upon by the Health Secretary to lead large-scale public health research, and hailed widely by her colleagues, both within the medical profession and the Civil Service, would be called upon to stop work as a result of one, innocuous life event. But at the age of fifty-two, when she married the Deputy Secretary of the Minister of Health, Sir Edward Rodolph Forber, Lane-Claypon's contract with the Department of Health was terminated, as married women were not permitted to work within the Civil Service.

Janet Lane-Claypon had taken Frognal Gardens into the twentieth century, proving herself eminently capable of professional prowess, but her career was curtailed by an outdated convention. The marriage bar had already been the subject of several government enquiries but would nevertheless continue to bring to an end a woman's contract within the Civil Service upon the event of her marriage until 1946, and in practice would persist for several decades beyond that in the form of temporary contracts for women, terminated on marriage. In this case alone, that practice was without doubt to result in a significant loss to science.

1 ALBANY STREET, REGENT'S PARK

Albany Street, lining the eastern edge of Regent's Park, dates back to the 1820s, when celebrated architect John Nash designed the street to screen the grand, park-fronting homes from the more commercial region of the city beyond. At less than a mile in length, it was to become home to artists, sculptors, writers, musicians and physicians throughout the nineteenth century, not least of which were celebrated physician, William Jenner, and poet, Edward Lear. Between 1827 and 1874, the street was also the site of the extravagant Colosseum, built to house a vast panoramic mural of the London cityscape.

By the turn of the century, the exclusively residential nature of the street was beginning to change. In 1906, Sir Charles Friswell established his extensive, five-storey 'House of Friswell', the country's largest car salesroom, at number 1, the point at which Albany Street meets Marylebone

Road. This was an impressive red-brick detached building, lined with arches and topped with turrets, sadly flattened during the Blitz, when the southern end of the street took two direct hits from the Luftwaffe. Friswell's had in any case ceased to operate by the early 1930s, but it was here, in an abandoned warehouse above a small car repair shop within the old Friswell's building, that the brains behind one of the country's most wildly successful home-spun talents engineered a momentous career first.

BERYL INGHAM
(1901–60)

In 1934 Beryl Ingham, a champion clog dancer from Lancashire with a successful song and dance act, a bonny face and a notoriously sharp tongue, joined a diminutive, toothy Lancastrian and a small cast and crew in an uninspiring one-room studio above a car repair shop on the corner of Albany Street, Regent's Park. On a shoestring budget and for a pitiful fee over which Ingham had wrangled, unsuccessfully, it was to be her first movie.

Hollywood, it was not. The noise the motor mechanics made in the workshop below was so pervasive, the director set up a bell to indicate when the cameras were rolling, a cue for the mechanics to head for a beer break at the nearest pub. The resulting movie, *Boots! Boots!*, was a stilted affair, shot predominantly from a single angle and generally poorly acted. Conversely, it proved wildly popular at the box offices across much of England.

The gawky lead actor making his big screen debut alongside Ingham was her husband, George Formby; his wife was formidable, a hurricane, a force of nature and was entirely responsible for Formby's rise to unprecedented success.

Formby's biographers have been quick to detail Ingham's universal unpopularity, presenting her as bossy, domineering, conniving and matriarchal. They cite the many who worked with her who subsequently demonised her for her omnipresence throughout her husband's career; certainly, she was backstage at every theatre, lurked on every movie set and even travelled with him to war zones.

Less well known was that Formby was entirely illiterate and unable to read music. In his dressing room, Ingham would help him learn his lines by rote, stepping in to help him manage any script changes and tuning his many banjos and ukuleles to different keys, labelling them with simple codes so that he knew which to play for each number. Her presence at his side, far from holding him back, was his lifeline. Those who knew the couple were well aware of this. Late in their marriage, after George confided to his friend, Tommy Trinder, that he was contemplating leaving Beryl, Trinder recalled having thought, 'It was like a blindman saying he was getting rid of his guide dog.'[7] George without Beryl was unthinkable.

For her part, sacrificing her own career in order to manage his, and happily playing the ogre in the process, seemed to come as no obvious burden. Ingham once admitted, '[George] hasn't had a row with anyone in showbusiness. I do all the battling. I don't care what they say about me; I *do* care what they say about George.'[8]

She gained a reputation as a fearsome foe to any of George's leading ladies, making demands of directors that were often unworkable. When a pretty 13-year-old Betty Driver (*Coronation Street*) made her screen debut in a cabaret scene in *Boots! Boots!*, Ingham insisted she was cut from the film, yelling, 'Either that kid goes, or I do!'[9] in front of the whole cast. The scene was reshot, with Ingham dancing the routine; Driver returned home to Manchester, crying all the way. Irene Bevan, step-daughter of Gracie Fields, and close friend of the Formbys, later recalled Ingham exclaiming, 'I don't care if she *was* only thirteen! She behaved like a floosy and I wasn't having any of it.'[10] In fact, this was to become something of a *modus operandi*; five years later, on the set of Formby's 1939

[7] BBC Television *40 Minutes*, Season 2, Episode 4: The George Formby Story produced by Ann Paul, Broadcast 1981 TRINDER.

[8] www.georgeformby.org

[9] From an interview with Betty Driver in *The South Bank Show*, Season 16, Episode 6: George Formby, 8 November 1992.

[10] Bret, David, *George Formby: An Intimate Biography of the Troubled Genius* (Lulu Press, 2014).

movie, *Come On George!*, the glamorous British star Pat Kirkwood found working with the Formbys an unhappy experience, in no small part due to Ingham's insistence that Kirkwood was 'deglamorised'[11] before appearing as Formby's love interest. She tried to insist Kirkwood's luscious locks were shorn and her wardrobe confined to unalluring costumes. Betty Driver summed it up: 'She was a very disliked lady, I'm afraid.'[12]

Regardless of her image and reputation in the industry, Beryl Ingham proved herself to be one of the most remarkable managers of the era. She made a succession of highly astute decisions on her husband's behalf, including having been the driving force behind his switch from stage to screen in 1934. A shrewd move: he became the biggest box-office draw in the UK for six successive years through the 1930s, finally signing a contract with Columbia in 1941 worth a staggering half a million pounds (sterling), making him the world's fifth biggest star, out-earning the likes of Bette Davis and Bing Crosby. Successive directors loathed her; some even tried to ban her from the set. None knew the extent to which her husband's performance depended on her presence.

She arranged a tour to South Africa in 1946 and resolutely refused to comply with demands made by National Party leader and key architect of Apartheid, Daniel François Malan, who insisted angrily on the Formbys performing only to white audiences. At Ingham's defiant instigation, they played to black audiences throughout the tour; she even had Formby pose with a 3-year-old child who had presented them with a box of chocolates. Malan was furious and had them thrown out of South Africa. Beryl, fearless, called him a 'horrible little man',[13] throwing in a few choice four-letter words by way of emphasis.

Formby owed his act, image, career and success to Beryl. On

---

[11] Pat Kirkwood: Obituary (*The Telegraph*, 29 December 2007).

[12] From an interview with Betty Driver in *The South Bank Show*, Season 16, Episode 6: George Formby, 8 November 1992.

[13] Bret, David, *George Formby: An Intimate Biography of the Troubled Genius* (Lulu Press, 2014).

their first encounter in the early 1920s, he had been a third-rate musical hall performer trying and failing to capitalise on his late father's stage legacy (his father's dishevelled, bowler-hatted, walking stick-twirling stage persona is said to have first influenced Charlie Chaplin). Beryl had honed his musicianship, smartened up his act and begun a lifelong process of compensating for his illiteracy. She confessed to having wanted to throw rotten tomatoes at him when she watched him on stage for the first time, and yet under her guidance, he rose to become the highest paid entertainer in the UK: he was commanding around £100,000 a year at the height of his career, at a time when the professional classes could expect to earn around £1,000. His appeal extended far beyond the working classes of the north of England from where he hailed: HM The Queen has always been a considerable fan and once confessed in correspondence to her secretary to knowing all the words to all his songs, even giving serious thought to becoming President of the George Formby Society. His funeral in March 1961 attracted a hundred and fifty thousand mourners.

Beryl Ingham was a powerhouse of a woman, much maligned by all who worked with her and yet undeterred. Days after her death from leukaemia in December 1960, the man to whom she had given almost forty years of her life, despite his endless affairs, betrayed her to the press, telling them life with Beryl had been 'hell' and crassly admitting to having lived a sexless marriage.

Biographer David Bret notes that in the scratchy, poorly shot and largely pitifully acted scenes filmed in the old warehouse on Albany Street in 1934, two performances stand out. Formby's, the first sight of the genius screen presence he would go on to develop, and Ingham's: a glimpse of quite how much she had sacrificed of her own career and ambition in order to maximise that of her husband.

The remarkable and triumphant managerial prowess behind the biggest British entertainer in history is worthy of memorial.

25 BEDFORD SQUARE, BLOOMSBURY

ADELAIDE ANNE PROCTER
(1825–64)

Adelaide Anne Procter was a British feminist, poet and philanthropist, born at 25 Bedford Square into a literary family who had strong connections with some of the leading literary figures of the era, including Charles Dickens, Elizabeth Gaskell, William Makepeace Thackeray, Dante Gabriel and Christina Rossetti and William Wordsworth. She showed literary prowess from an early age, submitting poems to Charles Dickens's weekly magazine under a pseudonym so that he would judge it on its own merits, rather than be influenced by the family friendship. He liked her work and asked that she submit regularly, which she continued to do for several years before Dickens finally discovered her true identity.

Procter's poetry garnered huge attention nationally, making her a household name and a best-seller, particularly once she was named as a favourite poet of Queen Victoria, but she directed a significant portion of the proceeds to charitable projects for women and children across London. She was a committed feminist, working with the Langham Place Group, by whom she was regarded as their 'animating spirit'.

12 QUEEN SQUARE, BLOOMSBURY

MARY SOMERVILLE
(1780–1872)

Mary Somerville was deprived of any education at all until the age of ten and then restricted to those curricula deemed suitable for her gender, and yet by adulthood she had proved herself a polymath, a gifted mathematician and astronomer, widely revered by the scientific community. Born in Jedburgh, Scotland, to Vice-Admiral Sir William George Fairfax, in childhood she had stumbled on an aptitude and passion for mathematics by chance, listening in on her brother's private mathematics tuition, and came to geometry circuitously, via lessons in perspective in art.

After her sister's untimely death, Somerville was forced to continue her studies covertly, forbidden to do so by her parents, who bought into perceived wisdom that academic pursuits were dangerous for women's health (to study required a rush of blood to the brain, the argument went; the impact of this on menstruating women was regarded as potentially critical to health and sanity). Later, encouraged by a more enlightened second husband, Dr William Somerville, with whom she lived on Queen Square, Mary Somerville proved wrong both her parents and the misconceptions to which they had pandered, coming to prominence as a mathematician and scientist while simultaneously raising four children. In 1835, she and Caroline Herschel were the first women ever appointed to the Royal Astronomical Society and Somerville later received an annual pension from the British government to fund her continued scientific research.

CHAPTER SEVEN

Islington

7 SOLEY TERRACE, ON THE SITE OF 60 GREAT PERCY STREET, AMWELL STREET, CLERKENWELL

In 1828, a brand new development of twenty-three terraced houses sprang up on Claremont Square along the southern edge of Great Percy Street, at its eastern junction with Amwell Street. It was a good site on which to build, as Clerkenwell supplied the city with fresh drinking water from its many springs. The development was named Soley or Solly Terrace. By 1831, most of the new homes were occupied, although with construction on Great Percy Street continuing around them, it would have been a noisy, dusty place to live.

Of the first run of nine houses from the corner with Amwell Street, only four survive today, numbers 72 to 66 Great Percy Street (once 1 to 4 Soley Terrace), the rest lost to the Blitz and post-war redevelopment. Number 7 is among those now lost, but had been one of the first to be occupied in 1829. It was home to a young Scottish journalist named Thomas Pringle and his wife, Margaret, both recently returned to the UK following an unsuccessful attempt to make a new life for themselves in South Africa. By chance, an article written by Pringle in Cape Town came to the attention of leading British abolitionists. It made a strong case for the abolition of the slave trade, and impressed the English abolitionists sufficiently to appoint Pringle secretary of the Anti-Slavery Society. So it was that in December 1829, the Pringles welcomed a new servant to their domestic staff: a tenacious, rheumatic woman, far from home, with a remarkable story that Pringle was determined to help her tell.

MARY PRINCE
(C. 1788–UNKNOWN)

The day Mary Prince joined the domestic staff at 7 Soley Terrace in December 1829 marked a significant turning point in her life. Though all too familiar with the work she was employed to do as a charwoman, the fact of her employment stood in marked contrast to the life she had lived until that point. The Pringles were kind and generous and treated her with the respect she deserved; moreover, they wanted to hear her story.

Prince told them she had been born into slavery in Bermuda in 1788, and was sold on from her mother during childhood. She had lived with a succession of masters, had sustained violence and brutality over many years and had the scars to prove it, her body ravaged with the marks of horse-whip and cat-o-nine-tails. Finally, she had been bought by a plantation owner from Antigua named John Adams Woods, who, she told the Pringles, had been the author of much of her scarring. Woods had raged when he discovered Prince had married in secret, a former slave-turned-freeman named Daniel James. She told how Woods had her beaten and then set about trying to end their marriage by inciting Prince to 'an instance of depravity'.

In 1828, she had travelled with Woods and his family to London, where the climate exacerbated her rheumatism, making it increasingly painful for her to carry out her laundry duties. As Prince's health deteriorated, tensions in the household reached a peak. Woods and his wife accused her of indolence and would later have a succession of witnesses (many of them slave owners themselves) testify in court to Prince's troublesome nature and disinclination to work. In any case, a slave too ill to work was of no value and so Woods provoked her, reminding her that slave-ownership was outlawed on English soil: in London, she was technically free to leave. Prince later recalled the moment, '[I] stood a long time before I could answer, for I knew that I was free in England, but did not know where to go, or how to get my living.' Freedom, she knew, came at a cost: if she were ever to return to Antigua to rejoin her husband, she would be Woods's property once more. Though alone in an alien, cold and dirty city, life within the Woods' household was no longer tolerable: she had to leave.

She took a risk on the only kindly face she had encountered in London, a shoeblack and knife sharpener named Mash, who had regularly visited the Woods' home. She pleaded with Mash and his wife to take her in, which they did. In their care, Prince experienced her first taste of the peace, dignity and respect she had lacked her entire life; Mash knew well enough the treatment she had endured, he had witnessed it himself at the Woods' home on several occasions. Exhausted and bed-ridden, Prince lived with the shoeblack and his wife for several months, and later wrote about them, 'they nursed me, and did all that lay in their power to serve me'.

Deeply moved by Prince's story, Pringle fought, unsuccessfully, for her formal emancipation so that she could return to her husband a free woman. The Anti-Slavery Society offered to buy her freedom from Woods but spitefully he refused that too; an acquaintance later told a court that Woods had admitted he may have been inclined to emancipate Prince had she returned with him to Antigua, but refused to do so at anyone else's interference.

Pringle recognised there was much political mileage to be gained in the unbearable detail of Prince's story and persuaded her to tell it to the nation in the form of a biographical pamphlet. In 1829 the trade in slaves had already been outlawed for twenty years but the owner-ship of those already enslaved in the colonies remained entirely legal, though the subject of bitter dispute. Pringle anticipated that Prince's story, told simply and honestly, would be an explosive weapon in the fight for abolition.

In the event, *The History of Mary Prince*, published in 1831 as tran-scribed by Pringle's friend, Susanna Strickland, offered an account of the reality of slavery as harrowing as he had anticipated. Written simply, in direct, first-person phrasing, Prince's words are as deeply moving today as they must have been to their nineteenth-century audience. The pamphlet was reprinted three times within the first year, reaching a wide audience and garnering crucial support for the abolitionary cause. For all that, it bears the marks too of the careful editing of a woman with nineteenth-century English sensibilities. What Strickland omitted from Prince's account is telling. The book wasn't intended to serve as a full testament to the life of a remarkable, tenacious and much-wronged woman so much as to stand as a piece of propaganda, truthful, well-intended, but edited to win as much support as possible.

What was omitted in the book was spoken from the witness stand before the King's Bench by Prince herself, recorded in court transcripts from the subsequent libel suit in which her former slave-master, John Adams Woods, sued Pringle for libelling him in the manuscript. Before a court filled with barristers, Prince retold her story, an uneducated woman whose life hadn't been her own for the first forty years. This time, she told her story unabridged. She told of the slave owner who kept her as his mistress for seven years, not allowing her in his home, but sleeping with her in a hut; of another who fooled her into believing he could help her win her emancipation, so long as she would sleep with him. The transcript records how the court laughed as she recounted the details; undeterred, she told her story.

It had taken enormous courage and strength of character to step out into the cold London air and carve out a 'free' life for herself, without a soul at her side. It took courage to present a petition to the British Parliament as she did in 1829, pleading for her liberation from John Adams Woods, the man who had horse-whipped her, attempted to force her into lewd acts in order to compromise her marriage and who ultimately refused either to free her, or sell her on out of his control, until a change in the law finally forced his hand in 1834. Mary Prince may have relied upon the hand of another to get her story into print, but she took a far from passive part in her own liberation.

Thomas Pringle died of tuberculosis in 1834, but lived just long enough to see abolition finally pass into law. John Adams Woods and his family left Antigua in 1830, to settle in Bloomsbury, an area which attracted significant numbers of those who grew rich from slavery. Immediately prior to abolition, slave inventories record that Woods had a total of 242 enslaved people living under his charge on his Antiguan plantation. He died in January 1836, sixteen months after abolition came into effect; in that time, he filed thirty separate claims seeking compensation from the British government for loss of 'property'. The vast majority were successful. He was awarded in excess of £18,200; according to the Bank of England inflation calculator, in 1835 this was the equivalent of somewhere in the region of £2.1 million today.

Mary Prince remained in the employment of the Pringles for a short while, but at the Woods v. Pringle libel case in 1833, gave her address as the Old Bailey. What became of her after abolition has been lost to time, though it seems likely she would have done whatever she could to return to her husband, Daniel James, in Antigua, a free woman at last.

Her struggle, her courage and her singular role in the final push for abolition bears memorial.

MARQUESS ROAD, CANONBURY

In 1919, Marquess Road, Canonbury, a crescent around the green space adjacent to St Paul's Church, was lined on both sides with a sweep of functional Victorian terraces. They were typical of the clusters of housing which had sprung up around the borough's prosperous Georgian heart in the second half of the nineteenth century, catering to a growing working-class population. Marquess Road escaped the Luftwaffe's bombing raids in the 1940s but was razed after the war to make way for a housing estate, the largest post-war housing project in the borough, completed in 1976. But in 1919, as the nation enjoyed its first taste of peace after the horrors of the Great War, one of the city's most courageous daughters moved into lodgings in a single room at number 68. Much of the story of her life is as lost today as the home in which she lived, but the story of her remarkable war survives.

DOROTHY LAWRENCE
(1896–1964)

In 1915, Dorothy Lawrence was dumped on the London Embankment by officers from Scotland Yard, clutching a guinea pig, gifted to her days earlier by the nuns from a French convent near the Somme. She had no home to which she could return and no family upon whom to call. In the preceding months, she had succeeded in pulling off the unthinkable; an unparalleled feat, which she had survived with her life and dignity intact. And yet back in her hometown, she was nonetheless without hope, her intentions mistrusted and her efforts thwarted by the strong arm of the Establishment. She can only have felt as if she had reached a nadir in what had already been a cruelly challenging life; in fact, there was worse to come.

She had been born and raised in North London by a single mother until she was orphaned in her early teens. Lone parenting was a rare phenomenon at the turn of the twentieth century and perhaps the resilience Dorothy was to exhibit as a young woman had been inherited from and modelled by her mother. At the age of thirteen, she gained a legal guardian, a senior and respectable figure within the Church of England, and was sent to live in Salisbury's Cathedral Close with a decent and honourable lady whom she would later name as her only friend. She was educated, lived in more comfort than anything she could previously have known in London, and had apparently every advantage. Yet just two years later, in 1911, at the age of fifteen, Dorothy returned to the capital to make her way in life alone.

She secured work as a journalist, a profession only recently opening its doors to women, albeit restricting them to the society and light entertainment columns. Dorothy aspired to more: she wanted to prove herself just as capable a journalist as the next man. When war broke out in 1914, she saw an opportunity. She approached every newspaper on Fleet Street, pitching the idea of taking her on as a war correspondent. Not one took her seriously, but *The Times*, at least, helped secure her a passport and gave her a cursory promise to look at her work in the unlikely event she managed to get herself to the Front.

From Calais, she passed six weeks trying to move among the troops in Paris and in the smaller towns beyond, looking for an angle to her story. Most whom she encountered misunderstood her mission, taking her to be a prostitute. Disillusioned, she came to see that to make progress, she would need to disguise her gender entirely. She confided in two English soldiers in Paris and persuaded them to set her up with a uniform, piece by piece. After casting off her petticoats, she bought a bike and muddied her complexion using a disinfectant named Condy's Fluid. Closer to the Front, she talked two Scottish Military Police into helping her shave off her long locks, completing the transformation. She bound her chest, donned her uniform and set herself up with new ID as Sapper Denis Smith. In the town of Albert, a Lancastrian Sapper named Tom Dunn took pity on her, helping her to shelter until he was moved up to the Front, at which point, finally, Dorothy went with him.

For ten days and nights, she lived and worked with the troops on the Front, joining a tunnelling company of the Royal Engineers as they dug beneath No Man's Land. When the conditions triggered a series of fainting fits, Lawrence decided to turn herself in, afraid that if her true identity and gender were to be uncovered while unconscious, her friend and ally, Tom Dunn, could be implicated and face court martial.

The problem facing the officers who now interrogated Lawrence was how to classify her actions. She had been arrested immediately, but a succession of six officers were at a loss as to how to proceed; what offence had she committed? A woman, in uniform, on the Front was such an anomaly: was she a spy, or a 'camp follower' – a prostitute? Having satisfied themselves she was neither, they were nonetheless stumped. In any case, they concluded, she would have to be detained; the Battle of Loos was imminent and a woman at the Front couldn't be trusted. They removed her to a convent in Saint-Omer for another fortnight, until she finally persuaded them to allow her to return to London.

By chance on the ferry home, she met suffragette Emmeline Pankhurst, in whom she confided. Emmeline insisted she tell her story back home in a series of lectures. The British authorities, however, had other ideas. Under no circumstances could they allow word to get out that a woman had smashed their security at the Front. They invoked the Defence of the Realm Act and forced Lawrence to sign away any right to publish her story until after peace had been declared.

Scotland Yard launched one last attempt to categorise her offence, but ultimately released her onto the banks of the Thames without charge, leaving her homeless, alone and with a crippling gag-order. For a single woman, dependent on her capacity to earn a living as a journalist, this was disastrous. She had begun to draft a book detailing her experiences, but in the next few months threw it on the fire.

Her experience in France was to stay with her for the rest of her days. She contracted septic poisoning, a souvenir from the trenches; worse, she was left with bizarre psychiatric symptoms, including a tremor so severe that at times it prevented her from writing. Post-traumatic stress disorder (PTSD), in 1919, wasn't a phenomenon anyone recognised or understood; least of all in a woman. She reflected later that the dangers she had faced as a lone woman in the company of thousands of men at the Front had extended beyond death, and expressed gratitude that the succession of men in whom she had confided had behaved impeccably and colluded in her mission. Importantly, every one of the soldiers she took into her confidence during her weeks in France had been sufficiently impressed by the strength of her conviction to offer her what help they could. She *had* achieved her goal and did so with her dignity intact.

With the end of the conflict in 1919, Lawrence had determined to publish her story. In her small rented rooms in Canonbury, she pulled her book together. *Sapper Dorothy* was published that year, though it caused only a minor ripple in the UK, Australia and the US, and was largely panned by critics. Within a few years, it had been forgotten. In 1920, the world wanted to roar, not reflect back on the dark days of the Western Front. No one wanted to hear about the remarkable efforts of a lone woman on a quest to prove her worth as a war correspondent.

With her PTSD growing increasingly impactful on her life, in 1925 at the age of twenty-nine, Lawrence finally sought medical help. She admitted to a doctor that the respectable figure from within the ranks of the Church of England who had first sent her as a teenager to live with Josephine Fitzgerald in Salisbury had subsequently raped her.

The physician failed to see before him a woman who had endured misogyny, gender discrimination and sexual exploitation throughout her life; who had been orphaned, raped, who had been forbidden from doing her job on the grounds of her gender, who had experienced the horrors of the Western Front and sustained lasting and incapacitating post-traumatic stress disorder and who had nonetheless fought for ten years to prove herself as a journalist. He saw only a woman without husband or respectable family, a woman with a history of unbecoming, attention-seeking behaviours and an array of bizarre nervous symptoms. He saw a woman who had deliberately courted danger, had been widely regarded with suspicion, written off as immoral, as either a spy or a prostitute, and who had been dismissed by the respectable press as 'a girlish freak'.

Unsurprisingly, Lawrence's allegations were met with ice-cold scepticism. She was incarcerated, first in Hanwell Lunatic Asylum and thereafter at Colney Hatch Lunatic Asylum in Friern Barnet, North London, where she languished until her death thirty-nine years later. Records indicate that although she sent for Josephine Fitzgerald, she received not a single visitor for the duration of that time.

Etched into the underbelly of London's history are countless, long-forgotten women who asked nothing more than to live the life they deserved and who were nonetheless crushed and silenced by the weight of the system stacked against them. All too often, their stories go untold. Against all odds, and at huge personal cost, Dorothy Lawrence told her story. For her courage and tenacity, for her journalism, she is remembered.

CHAPTER EIGHT

Hackney

HOLLY VILLAGE, HIGHGATE

In the heart of Highgate, in the London Borough of Hackney, sits the gothic hamlet of Holly Village, rich with turrets, spires, gables and towers. Finished lavishly in 1865 with the carvings of the finest Italian stonemasons, every thought was given to ensure the comfort of those living in the twelve homes, arranged as four detached houses and eight semi-detached cottages. Dust chutes were built into the floors, for instance, so that dust could be swept into the cellars. Holly Village has long been home to members of London's wealthy professional classes, but had been commissioned with vision and compassion by Victorian London's most prolific philanthropist, whose intention was that they should house the staff in the comfort of her Highgate estate.

ANGELA BURDETT-COUTTS
(1814–1906)

Sometimes, great wealth falls into the right hands. In 1837, at the age of twenty-three, Angela Burdett-Coutts gathered with her many relatives for the reading of the will of her late step-grandmother, Harriet Mellon, widow of the wealthy banker, Thomas Coutts. Harriet had spent her latter years quietly scrutinising her late husband's grandchildren. To the surprise of everyone present, Angela was named sole inheritor, coming into a fortune of £1.8 million. Overnight, she became the wealthiest woman in England and the talk of the nation. As *Punch Magazine* observed, 'The world set to work, match-making, determined to unite the splendid heiress to somebody'.

The splendid heiress, however, had other ideas and embarked instead upon a life crammed with foresight, imagination and generosity. Burdett-Coutts first invested in scientific advancement, financing the construction of Charles Babbage's groundbreaking 'calculating engine', the world's first computer. The same year, she befriended an author; a man so giddy with the success of his first two novels, *The Pickwick Papers* and *Oliver Twist*, that he was said to 'sparkle'. Charles Dickens would later name Angela's greatest quality: 'seeing clearly with kind eyes'.

Burdett-Coutts then cast those kind eyes on the city's least fortunate: the slum-dwellers. In an inspired move, she converted some of the city's oldest burial grounds into beautiful gardens so that the capital's most impoverished children had places in which they could play freely: London's first playgrounds. It would be almost twenty years before anyone else in the world would imagine a similar plan. She employed an army of travelling teachers to home-school the children of the slums, and later funded the Ragged School Union. It was Angela's money which financed the creation of the National Society for the Prevention of Cruelty to Children in 1884. She tackled, too, the worst of the East London slums, tearing them down and building clean, safe, low-rent housing in their place. And she had the vision to bring about the economic regeneration of the area, building the Columbia Road Market in Bethnal Green in 1869, a community hub where locals could trade their way out of discomfort.

To the bewilderment of her close friend, the Duke of Wellington (to whom she proposed marriage several times, despite his significant age), Burdett-Coutts sank more money into a scheme for fallen women, headed by Dickens. Nuria House was a safe house in rural Shepherd's Bush, where female thieves, thugs and prostitutes could be rehabilitated with kindness and generosity. In the 1860s, she worked with Dickens in the planning of another innovative housing project, the gothic masterpiece, Holly Village, built into the grounds of her family estate, Holly Lodge, on Highgate's West Hill. She and Dickens were said to have spent long hours deliberating over every aspect of the project, calling upon the services of architect, Henry Darbishire, who also built the philanthropic housing on London's Peabody estate. Opinions vary about the early tenants of the houses built on Holly Lodge – by the early twentieth century, most were wealthy professionals – but it seems Burdett-Coutts and Dickens had intended the project to house the staff employed on her estate. Typically, she opened the gardens of the village as a playground for local children.

Burdett-Coutts' generosity knew no bounds and in many cases she made donations anonymously. All were based on her driving principle that the poor wanted opportunity rather than charity. Her philanthropy extended to animal welfare too: her money bolstered the fledgling London charity, 'The Temporary Home for Lost and Starving Dogs', now the Battersea Dogs & Cats Home. In 1871, the woman Prince Edward (later Edward VII) described as 'the most remarkable woman in the kingdom',[14] second only to his mother, was rewarded with a peerage, making Baroness Burdett-Coutts the first woman to have risen to the ranks of the aristocracy, as a reward for a life well lived.

Burdett-Coutts lived most of her life with her beloved governess, Hannah Brown, until Brown's death in 1878; both are depicted in stylised form on the gates of Holly Village. Brown's death left Burdett-Coutts, now in her mid-sixties, heart-broken; three years later, she caused much controversy when, at the age of sixty-seven, she married her 29-year-old American private secretary, William Lehman Ashmead Bartlett. The marriage was a remarkable one for the era, and not simply because of the age difference: unusually, Bartlett took his wife's name. Angela and William Burdett-Coutts spent twenty-five happy years together, until her death, during which time they entertained lavishly and, after which, William continued her philanthropic work.

Angela Burdett-Coutts died on 30 December 1906, having donated £3 million to good works over her lifetime. In the days before her funeral in Westminster Abbey, in January 1907, a staggering thirty thousand Londoners came to pay their respects to the woman they knew as the 'Queen of the Poor'.

---

[14] *Encyclopaedia Britannica, 11th Edition, Vol 4, Part 4,* 2007.

Hoxton Hall, Hoxton Street, Hoxton

The earliest origins of the Hoxton Hall community centre date back to 1863, when it first opened as Macdonald's Music Hall, one of two built during the second half of the century in what was then an almost exclusively working-class area. Its rival, the Britannia, was well known across the city, praised by the likes of Charles Dickens, who compared it favourably to Milan's Opera House, La Scala, but Macdonald's was a saloon-style place, catering to those who lived in Hoxton's extensive Victorian slums. With living conditions meagre, cramped and comfortless, the public houses – and now Macdonald's Music Hall – offered the people of Hoxton the only environment in which they could pass what little leisure time they had. The resulting spread of alcohol consumption, however, became a source of alarm and police complaints about the fall-out on the streets led to the closure of the music hall in 1871. Hoxton Hall then became home to an altogether different occupant, the Blue Ribbon Gospel Temperance Mission. The Blue Ribbon group's efforts to offer the people of Hoxton an alternative to the pubs attracted the considerable philanthropic attention of one of London's most remarkable women, a passionate social reformer and the city's most renowned undercover journalist.

Olive Christian Malvery
(1876/7–1914)

Sometimes, before a city can embrace change, it needs to see itself through the lens of an informed outsider. At the turn of the twentieth century, London was in a place of confluence. Victorian industrial and imperial expansion had brought as much shade as light to the city and the socio-economic changes the new century would bring were yet to reveal themselves. The moralistic swagger of nineteenth-century London's privileged classes lingered in many quarters, so that too many of the 'haves' consoled themselves and their consciences that the uglier sides of life in the city were largely self-inflicted by a 'deserving poor'.

Olive Christian Malvery was precisely the catalyst the city's upper middle classes needed to bring about a vital change in perception. Raised in the Punjab, of Anglo-Indian parentage, Malvery was well schooled in the ways of the British privileged classes. After her parents separated, still in Lahore, Olive and her brother were immersed in the very British ways of her Anglican maternal grandparents so when she found herself on British soil at the tender age of nineteen or twenty, a student at the Royal School of Music, she was able to fall seamlessly into line with societal expectations.

Enormously charismatic, Malvery soon made a name for herself in some of London's most favoured parlours, giving musical recitals and regaling her audiences with tales of exotic British India. She discovered a talent for story-telling, but gleaned something too about what lay beneath the surface of some of the delicate sensibilities of those she entertained. London's finest men and women, she came to see, were not only ignorant of the grim reality of life for those she described as 'the submerged tenth'; they were, it appeared, *wilfully* so. It suited them, then, not to shine a spotlight on anything that would offend their delicacy. This 'false modesty' became something Malvery was determined to address.

She embarked upon a remarkable career as a journalist with a social conscience. Writing for *Pearson's Magazine*, addressing a monied, educated middle-class professional audience, she was able to capitalise on a brand new era in pan-Atlantic journalism, one in which named journalists drew a devoted readership for the first time, and which could embrace photo-journalism, thanks to the very latest printing technology.

For more than a decade, Malvery made a name for herself for her biting social exposés. She used plain language, tackled difficult issues and brought a gravitas to her columns in a remarkable way: she worked undercover. Over the years, she experienced first-hand the harsh realities of those spending long hours simply trying to survive. She slept rough, lodged in filthy boarding houses, worked long, arduous hours as costermonger, flower girl, street singer, factory girl, waitress and barmaid. She rose when her companions rose, worked as they worked, ate as they ate. And then told her readership every detail.

She brought theatre to her writing. Edition after edition of *Pearson's Magazine* revealed her dressed in the garb of the women among whom she had been immersed. Some modern commentators have accused Malvery of titillating her readers. Her 1912 work, *The White Slave Market*, for instance, which looked at the sex-trade in British prostitutes sent overseas, lingered in part on the soft wave of a kiss-curl, the rosebud lips and the pink negligee of a young prostitute, but Malvery knew what she was doing. She wanted to bring about a sea change in opinion and to do that she needed to make certain London's enfranchised were paying attention.

Her words in *The White Slave Market* carry a strikingly modern message, and one only a woman of her influence and experience could have carried. 'We are not aiming at anything so foolish as to the abolition of prostitution,' she wrote, 'for as long as the world lasts prostitution will last also.' What she urged instead was something altogether more arresting: 'we must organise and arrange that particular trade'. This Edwardian beauty, wife of a US diplomat, beloved in parlours across London, called in plain terms in 1912 for the regulation of the sex industry.

Her work with the costermongers of the East End left her with another lasting sense too. A passionate supporter of the Women's Temperance movement, Malvery began to see that for London's factory girls and costermongers, there was no social alternative to the beer houses of the East End slums. Days were lived from one to the next, with no thought for laying down a different future. Extended families lived out their days and nights in tiny single rooms, 'no larger than a good cupboard', which served as sleeping quarters, scullery, kitchen and storeroom: little incentive for hearty family nights in around a warm hearth. In the precious few hours of the week not spent toiling, Malvery saw that there was really only one environment in which life, love and leisure could be played out: the public houses. Though she despised the demon drink as much as the next self-respecting Edwardian Christian woman, hers was no inward-thinking, detached moral judgement. She realised that if London's poorest classes were to be persuaded off the drink, they needed a viable alternative to the pub. A place that enabled a gathering of 'wholesome, big-hearted friends'; a place of 'intelligent entertainment', and crucially, a place 'where all sermonising or religious lessons were sternly deleted'. Fun and companionship then; just without the liquor.

Malvery threw herself into supporting a growing social movement centred on Hoxton Hall. She gave her time and funds to the growth of a youth movement based at the hall, known as the Girls' Guild and the Lads' Club. She used her social connections to encourage fund-raising soirees, which London's elite attended in droves. Thanks to her tireless advocacy and fund-raising, Hoxton Hall was extended, with social, medical, educational and domestic facilities designed to open the doors on an entirely new life for the area's youth.

Within a decade, she became a celebrity. Her wedding, to the Scot, Archibald Mackirdy, a well-connected US Consul to Muscat, Persia, was covered in the society columns of all the London papers. Malvery appeared in print, strikingly beautiful in a pure white Indian sari and veil; but she *used* her wedding to make a powerful statement. On the guest list were a thousand East End costermongers and prostitutes. Her bridal bouquet of a dozen white roses was a gift from the flower sellers she had befriended while working undercover. At her side her bridesmaids were all East End child flower sellers. After a brief cake-cutting ceremony, the bride and groom retired for a reception at none other than Hoxton Hall.

Though Malvery and her husband made a comfortable life for themselves and their three children in rural Sussex, she never lost touch with the needs of the people of the East End. She was a product of the Empire, a woman entirely in touch with British society, at ease within its mores, yet boldly idiosyncratic and marginal enough to use her charisma to name some of British society's most uncomfortable truths. She embraced Christian morality and the Women's

Temperance movement whole-heartedly, but was never insular in her outlook, throwing herself into learning the complexities of what drove the women of London to drink or prostitution. Crucially, she didn't shy from suggesting a path to change that was entirely ahead of its day.

58A GELDESTON ROAD, CAZENOVE

Geldeston Road lies on the outskirts of the Northwold and Cazenove Conservation area, an area of Hackey that is rich with late Victorian sub-urban housing, built for the middle classes. At the turn of the twentieth century, the five-room flat at number 58a was home to a travelling rope salesman named Harry and his wife, Jessie, a headmistress at a school for learning disabled children. It was here in 1909 that Jessie gave birth to one of the nation's best-loved actresses.

JESSICA TANDY
(1909–94)

Jessica Tandy's professional career began unceremoniously at the age of eighteen in a small, back-room theatre in Soho, in a production of *The Manderson Girls*. Her meagre wage had to cover the cost of her five costumes. At that point in her career she was, in her own words, 'a graceless lump'; even her own two brothers, she once recalled, had complained whenever their mother insisted they include Jessica in their home-spun plays. It wasn't a promising start.

If Tandy felt she lacked the elegance of an *ingénue*, however, she more than compensated with her vigour and persistence. In 1932, having started to land West End roles, she gave a breakthrough performance in Christa Winsloe's *Children in Uniform*, moving her audiences and proving herself an actress of considerable talent. It led her to major stage roles opposite the leading actors of the day, including John Gielgud and Laurence Olivier. In 1940, with a failed marriage to British actor Jack Hawkins behind her, Jessica moved to the US with her 6-year-old daughter, Susan. A second marriage, to the wealthy Hollywood actor, Hume Cronyn, in 1942 opened the door to the movie industry and she began to land a series of small roles. When nothing of any substance was forthcoming, she became disheartened, and more than once contemplated quitting the business, but in the end her dogged resilience paid off. In 1946, a stage role brought her to the attention of one of America's finest playwrights, Tennessee Williams, at precisely the right moment. Williams was in the process of casting the inaugural production of *A Streetcar Named Desire* and Tandy struck him as the perfect Blanche DuBois. She proved a great choice, playing to critical acclaim, winning a Tony for the role, and finally solidifying her reputation in the US as a gifted actress.

Tandy's humble origins and faltering start to her professional career would have felled many less hardy actors, but those who knew her testified to her limitless energy and passion for work: she continued to work on television and movie roles right up until the last twelve months of her life, even after having been diagnosed with ovarian cancer in 1990. The 'graceless lump' ended her career having performed in more than a hundred stage roles and sixty screen appearances, and set a new theatrical record when, at the age of eighty in 1989, she became the oldest actress ever to have won an Academy Award, for her role as the prickly Southern Jewish widow in *Driving Miss Daisy*.

For a life well lived, Tandy is worthy of commemoration.

45 AMHURST PARK (NOW RAZED), STAMFORD HILL, HACKNEY

HELEN BAMBER
(1925–2014)

At the age of twenty, Helen Bamber volunteered with a humanitarian mission that was to alter the course of her life. She joined the Jewish Relief Unit, going into Bergen-Belsen concentration camp with a team to help with the rehabilitation of survivors, later working with orphaned children liberated from Auschwitz. It was the start of a seventy-year career dedicated to supporting the victims of human rights abuses, human trafficking, domestic violence and torture. She was the first chair of the medical arm of Amnesty International in the UK and later founded Freedom From Torture, working with UK-based survivors.

Bamber spent her childhood living with her extended family at the home of her uncle, Michael Balmuth, in Amhurst Park, North London.

3 GORE ROAD, SOUTH HACKNEY

CATHERINE BOOTH
(1829–90)

Catherine Booth was a devout Methodist Christian with a passionate belief in the power of preaching and a fervent social conscience. She also had to battle a debilitating timidity and anxiety about public speaking and a gender-restrictive attitude towards female preachers in order to pursue her calling. Born in Derbyshire, she came to Brixton with her family in 1844 and later married preacher, William Booth, with whom she co-founded the Salvation Army in South London in 1865. The couple moved into 3 Gore Road in 1868 where they raised their children for the next twelve years.

Catherine had been a reserved child and although adulthood had done nothing to ease her shyness, she felt her calling was not simply to observe her faith but also to preach. When Booth forbade her to preach, believing it inappropriate for women to do so, she carefully constructed a sound theological argument to convince him, citing Bible passages in support of her argument, and succeeded in changing his mind. Battling her extreme shyness, she shattered the social convention that women not speak out in public gatherings and became a renowned preacher in her own right. She was an ardent activist for social reform and published widely on the subject of fair working conditions and equal pay for women in the match-making factories of London's East End.

4 CHRISTOPHER STREET, SHOREDITCH

HELEN TAYLOR
(1831–1907)

British feminist, writer and actress Helen Taylor was born on Christopher Street, Shoreditch, to John Taylor, druggist, and radical political thinker, Harriet Taylor Mill *(see also page 19)*. Harriet instilled in her daughter a love of education and a desire to fight for feminist issues. After the death of her mother in 1858, Taylor became companion and aide to her step-father, John Stuart Mill, who credited her with having been collaborative in his later works, including *The Subjection of Women* (1869).

After Mill's death, Taylor became an active promoter of social and gender equality, was known as a powerful orator and accepted an invitation to become a member of the London School Board, where she pushed for the wholesale reform of the notorious Industrial Schools. She was a passionate and active supporter of the campaign for women's suffrage and in 1885 became the first woman to stand for Parliamentary election, campaigning on a socialist platform that attracted much controversy. Her nomination was rejected by the returning officer on the grounds of her gender.

CHAPTER NINE

Haringey

105 *FROBISHER ROAD, HORNSEY*

By the late decades of the nineteenth century, much of Hornsey was still undeveloped, privately owned land with a slower rate of construction in comparison to other regions of the capital. A spray of housing was thrown up in the 1870s around Horney's railway stations, designed to attract the professional middle classes. Then at the turn of the century, generous terraced and semi-detached housing was built to cater for a less wealthy white-collar population who made up a sizeable proportion of working residents on the 1911 census. The area's green expanses and parkland were preserved, however, keeping Hornsey's population low and earning it a reputation as 'Healthy Hornsey'. It was, then, the perfect suburb in which to raise a family at the start of the twentieth century; little surprise that George and Alice Lingstrom and their three daughters chose to move out of Chelsea and make their home in a four-bedroom, bay-fronted terrace at 105 Frobisher Road in 1900. Youngest in the family was Freda, who was just six years old when her family arrived on Frobisher Road. Many of her childhood memories would have been formed at the house; after the Second World War, Freda's artistry, imagination and creativity would come to change the lives of children across the nation.

FREDA LINGSTROM
(1893–1989)

By the early 1920s, Freda Lingstrom was still a young woman but already had a great deal of experience behind her. She had trained at Central School of Art, fallen in love, had her heart broken when her fiancé was killed in the First World War, ventured out to live alone in London and launched a promising career as an emerging designer. In the telephone directories of the decade, she listed herself as an artist, moving into and out of a succession of addresses across Holborn and

Paddington, and she had been the talent behind a series of travel post-ers for London Underground and the Norwegian Travel Board. The phase of her life which was to prove her greatest legacy, however, was yet to start.

In 1940, having built a solid reputation as a designer, Lingstrom took a career change, bringing her designer's eye for detail and her artist's creativity to the BBC. Very quickly, she was drawn into the BBC's work for children, contributing to a children's periodical called *Junior*, along with George Orwell and Maria Bird. Bird would become Lingstrom's lifelong companion, the two drawn together by their common loss of a fiancé during the war. They would also pioneer a new era of broadcasting for children.

When Lingstrom moved over into children's radio broadcasting it was still characterised by dry, educational schools broadcasting. She came to see that there was a need for something altogether new: cre-ative programming specifically designed for early years. The result was a revolution in British broadcasting: *Listen With Mother* aired for the first time in 1950. This was storytime on the radio, targeting chil-dren under five years of age. An instant success, it led to Lingstrom's first television commission, *Andy Pandy*, which first aired in July 1950. The programme was an experiment, aired in a slot tucked in between women's television programmes, but it proved a huge success with mothers and children alike.

Buoyed by her first television success, Lingstrom was appointed director of children's television in 1951, leading a team of seven produc-ers. In contrast to the comfortable worlds she created on screen, she earned a reputation for being somewhat stern within the BBC, where she was rumoured to have been called 'The Old Cough Drop' behind her back. The early BBC had been almost exclusively about variety: her fiercely intellectual approach to children's programming was new and her uncompromising reputation was a means of being taken seriously within what was a predominantly male institution. Certainly, she fought hard within the BBC to raise the profile of children's television, and to increase budgets accordingly, and was responsible for a string of enduring successes, including *The Flowerpot Men* in 1952, and the television transfer of her radio success, *Watch With Mother*, in 1953. Later, she would be responsible for *Crackerjack, Rag, Tag and Bobtail* and *Sooty and Sweep*, as well as for some of the best-loved faces of early children's television, including Johnny Morris of *Animal Magic* and *Tales of the Riverbank* fame.

She retired from television in 1956, but continued to live with Maria Bird, with whom she collaborated on many of her programmes, until Bird's death in the 1980s. Throughout that time, both Bird and Lingstrom wrote a succession of children's books featuring their television characters, including Andy Pandy, Bill and Ben and The Woodentops. By the time of Lingstrom's death in 1989, children's television had evolved beyond recognition, from her early, fifteen-minute experiment, broadcast in the middle of women's daytime programming, to what had become a driving force of mainstream culture and education.

CHAPTER TEN
Redbridge

'EVERSLEY', GLENGALL ROAD, WOODFORD

Woodford, in the London borough of Redbridge, was a seventeenth- and eighteenth-century retreat for wealthy bankers, ship builders and retired East India Company captains, who built many vast country homes close enough to reach the capital with ease by coach and horse. The international travels of many of its residents accounted for an unusually high proportion of black servants recorded in family archives from this era. With the arrival of the railway in 1856, linking Woodford to London, Woodford expanded significantly, with most of the eighteenth-century country homes razed to make way for a crop of Victorian residences, built to house an increasing number of well-to-do middle-class commuters. 'Eversley' was one of a row of generous bay-fronted detached late-Victorian villas on Glengall Road, given names rather than numbers. By 1918, this was the home of a family of four, the youngest of whom was an infant who would grow into a diminutive woman with high aspirations.

JOAN HUGHES
(1918–93)

Joan Hughes's life serves to remind us all that dedication, application and nerves of steel can see a childhood dream become reality. She grew up in an era which saw the first commercial passenger flights available in Britain: Imperial Airways was launched in 1924, with wooden bi-planes giving way to metallic monoplanes, offering space and style and increasingly long-haul travel options. From an early age, Joan was hooked and became the youngest woman ever to have gained her pilot's licence on her seventeenth birthday in 1935.

In 1938, Hughes signed up for the Civil Air Guard, a government subsidy scheme which enabled her to train on a variety of different aircraft at a reduced cost, in exchange for offering military assistance to the Royal Air Force in the event of a military emergency. In 1940, she was one of the celebrated 'First Eight' – eight experienced female pilots signed up as Test Pilots by the Air Transport Auxiliary. At only 5 feet 2 inches, and of very slight frame, her capacity to handle what were known as the 'Heavies', the four-engine planes such as Stirling and Hurricanes, was met with a broad scepticism, but before too long, Hughes's flight record stood for itself and by the end of the war, she had clocked up impressive hours in the air without ever losing an aircraft. Moreover, by 1944, she was the only woman training male and female pilots to fly all types of four-engine planes at the Advanced Flying Training School at White Waltham. In 1945 she was made MBE in acknowledgement of her contribution to the work of the ATA.

After the war, Joan continued to work as a flight instructor, gaining her RAF wings in 1954 and later joining the British Airways Flying Club in Buckinghamshire in 1961. By this point in her career, she had gained experience in flying a huge variety of aircraft and was introduced by an acquaintance to an entirely new world: that of a movie stunt pilot. Hughes was in the cockpit of several memorable flight scenes in a number of British films, including *Those Magnificent Men in Their Flying Machines*, and famously flying a Tiger Moth under a motorway bridge near High Wycombe as stunt pilot for Lady Penelope in the 1968 big screen version of the television series, *Thunderbirds*.

Hughes's passion for flight was the driving force of her life: she never married, claiming it would interfere with her flying. When she retired in 1985, she had clocked up 11,800 hours in her logbook, survived several hair-raising scrapes in the air, had shattered gender preconceptions about flying and earned the respect of all with whom she had come into contact.

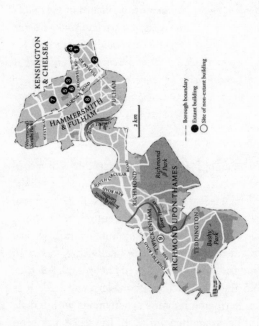

- — Borough boundary
- ● Extant building
- ○ Site of non-extant building

KENSINGTON & CHELSEA

1 Gertrude Bell (1868–1926), 95 Sloane Street, Knightsbridge SW1X 9PQ.
2 Margaret Damer Dawson (1873–1920), 10 Cheyne Row, Chelsea SW3.
3 Joan Beauchamp Procter (1897–1931), 11 Kensington Square, Kensington W8 5HE.
4 Judy Garland (1922–69), 4 Cadogan Lane, Belgravia SW1X.
5 Emilia Jessie Boucherett (1825–1905), 9 Upper Phillimore Gardens, Chelsea W8 7HF.
6 Rebecca Clarke (1886–1979), 12 Abingdon Mansions, Abingdon Road, Kensington W8 6AD.
7 Madame Blavatsky (1831–91), 17 Lansdowne Road, Holland Park W11 3LL.

HAMMERSMITH & FULHAM

8 Evelyn Cheesman (1881–1969), 4 Fairholme Road, Fulham W14 9JX.

RICHMOND UPON THAMES

9 Lady Mary Wortley Montagu (1689–1762), Saville Road, Twickenham TW1 4BQ.

HILLINGDON

10 Kathleen Lonsdale (1903–1971), 121 Station Road, (now razed), West Drayton UB7 7ND.
11 Louisa Nottidge (1802–1858), Moorcroft Park, Hartington Road, Hillingdon UB8 3HD.

134

CHAPTER ELEVEN

Kensington & Chelsea

95 SLOANE STREET, KNIGHTSBRIDGE

Sloane Street has always been opulent, since its early days as an exclusive Georgian out-of-town estate called Hans Town, where Jane Austen had pored over her manuscript for Sense and Sensibility. *By the late nineteenth century a sweep of later Victorian mansion homes on Sloane Street had prompted a corresponding rise in high-end drapers, tailors and milliners in adjoining Knightsbridge. Benjamin Harvey opened his first store here in 1831, on the corner of Sloane Street and Knightsbridge, still the spot at which its descendant, Harvey Nichols, stands today.*

By the 1890s, Sloane Street and its environs was one of the most fashionable addresses in London, but at number 95, positioned in the middle of the row facing Cadogan Place Gardens, lived a cerebral young woman fresh from her studies at Oxford. Knightsbridge would fail to hold her attention and she would embark upon a life of adventure, succumbing to the pull of her wanderlust and sharing her experiences in published travel journals, penned during brief stays on Sloane Street.

GERTRUDE BELL
(1868–1926)

Gertrude Bell was a woman of remarkable contrasts. She was a fearless trailblazer, whose knowledge, experience and opinion of Middle Eastern politics, people and culture was valued by the British government above all others in what was otherwise an entirely male world. In her youth, she scaled the world's highest mountains, trekked solo across Persia, led the Arab Office (the British intelligence service in the Middle East) during the First World War and helped map, define, construct and scaffold the construction of modern-day Iraq. It is said that in the region her name remains synonymous with female strength, while that of her contemporary, T. E. Lawrence, has been largely forgotten. And yet for all that, she embraced almost entirely the gender-specific expectations of the day, taking a strong stance against the women's suffrage movement and maintaining a strictly platonic relationship with the love of her life over many years because he was a married man.

Bell was born into a wealthy merchant family in the North East. Fiercely intelligent, she was the first woman ever awarded a First class honours degree in modern history at Oxford. After graduating, however, her family decided she needed a new kind of education, one they hoped would rid her of what they feared had become 'too Oxfordy' a manner. In 1892, she was sent on her first voyage to the Middle East to stay with an uncle who was British Ambassador in Tehran, Iran. It was to prove a turning point in her life.

Bell immersed herself in the experience and in so doing, fell in love with adventure. Back home, at the family's London residence on Sloane Street, she tried to retain the excitement of her travels by compiling a journal, which was published two years later in 1894 under the title, *Persian Pictures*. But her appetite for travel, adventure and risk meant London couldn't detain her for long. She discovered a passion for mountaineering, scaling Mont Blanc, La Meije and the Bernese Alps, with at least one peak, Gertrudspitz, named after her.

Gertrude pursued with vigour a growing love of archaeology, embarking on digs across Europe and the Middle East and becoming increasingly esteemed in the field, thanks to her several scholarly papers. She worked with some of the era's leading archaeologists and would first meet T. E. Lawrence in 1913 on an archaeological dig. Her reputation earned her an appointment to the Royal Geographical Society in London, where she was able to train in surveying techniques.

She would feel the pull of the Middle East for most of her life, crossing Arabia more than a dozen times, mapping formerly uncharted territories and moving freely among the peoples of many tribes, gaining the trust of many tribal leaders as she did so. Wherever she travelled, she wrote copiously in letters to her father and stepmother, kept journals and maintained an intricate photographic record. Her wealth supported a lifestyle abroad that would have been entirely unthinkable at home and began to set her apart from other British women of the age; consequently she gained a reputation in England for being remote and unapproachable. In contrast, those who knew her well described her in an entirely different light, as charismatic, impassioned and irrepressible: Vita Sackville-West wrote that she admired Bell's 'gift of making everyone feel suddenly eager, of making you feel that life was full and rich and exciting',[15] And the great love of her life, Major Charles Doughty-Wylie, was appalled by her threat to take her own life if ever he were to lose his in war and wrote her a passionate letter, urging that suicide was an unthinkable end for 'so free and brave a spirit'.

At the outbreak of the First World War, Bell had learned to converse fluently in Arabic, Persian, French, German, Turkish and Italian; she was an expert in the terrain, the people who populated it, their culture, traditions and politics. Significantly, she had made an extensive and perilous trek through what is now Saudi Arabia, territory that would become central to British interests during the war. Her expertise proved too valuable to overlook and saw Bell the only British woman raised to political office during the war. When the war ended, she attended the Paris Peace Conference. She took a pivotal role in the reorganisation of the Middle East, urging that Faisal be crowned king of the new state of Mesopotamia and all but single-handedly drawing up the borders of modern-day Iraq. Iraq became her passion – she was appointed by Faisal to the position of honorary director of antiquities, leading many archaeological digs and inviting in many more from overseas, and establishing the Museum of Baghdad in which to house the finds. The future of the new state, she urged, lay in its history: she convinced King Faisal that the uneasy combination of peoples who now found themselves to be Iraqi could be bound to a new national identity by way of a strong emphasis on their shared past.

During her lifetime, Bell divided opinion; posthumously, when her step-mother published Gertrude's extensive correspondence with

---

[15] Sackville-West, Vita, *A Passage to Teheran* (Tauris Parke Paperbacks, 2007).

her father, what had once been private thoughts on the region were made public and in consequence, many more came to mistrust her motivation. Indeed some Iraqis regarded her as 'The Spy', the face of the British establishment, while others referred to her respectfully as 'Al-Khatun' (The Lady), or raised her higher still, with the title, 'Umm Al-Muminin': Mother of the Faithful, a title formerly given to the wife of the Prophet Muhammad.

Travel had given Bell a freedom beyond the reach of other women of the age; it enabled her to reject the pressure to conform to the restrictive gender roles of the society in which she was born. At the same time, her opinionated stance on many issues of the day, not least her scathing position on the role of women within politics and on women's suffrage in particular, was grounded very much in the era and has therefore set her apart from any lasting regard as a feminist icon.

Bell voiced strident views on the future of the Middle East; on the formation of a strong and united Iraq, ruled by Faisal, which she insisted should include the Kurdish people; on what she saw as the incapacity of the region to succeed without British guidance, and on the role archaeology should play in securing that future. Many of her opinions on the way forward for Iraq were to be revisited, decades later, by the dictator Saddam Hussein, adding to the controversy with which her legacy is regarded.

And yet in pursuing her fascination with the region, immersing herself in the people, the history, the languages and the traditions, Bell created a role for herself that differed from that of almost any other woman in Britain at the time. In the process, she lived a life she could not otherwise have gained access to, carving out a name for herself in the fields of archaeology, mountaineering, exploration, espionage, cartography, politics and international diplomacy. Her extensive and detailed maps of previously uncharted regions, marked with railway lines, wells and details of those tribes that were friendly and those more hostile, proved invaluable to the Allied war effort during the First World War and, crucially, enabled her friend, T. E. Lawrence, to undertake his celebrated work. Lawrence has since been largely forgotten in the Middle East; Gertrude Bell, by contrast, is said to be one of the few British representatives remembered with any affection.

In some of the letters Bell wrote towards the end of her life, her driving motivation is made clear: she wanted neither wealth, which she had in any case, nor fame, which she found to be of no comfort. Rather, she hoped that her physical and intellectual accomplishments would bring with them a sense that she had earned her place in history and that she could become what she described as 'A Person'.

The career which began in her home in Sloane Street with a series of personal travel journals which she had no initial thought to publish grew into a remarkable, trailblazing life which shattered all contemporary expectations about the manner in which a woman should live and which left a lasting legacy more than worthy of commemoration.

10 CHEYNE ROW, CHELSEA

Cheyne Row is an unassuming Georgian three-storey terrace, a short stroll from Chelsea's Albert Bridge, described by Walter H. Godfrey in his 1913 Survey of London as 'scarcely warrant[ing] detailed description'. In fact, the two houses either side of number 10 at the time of Godfrey's survey stood empty, though the comings and goings at the house in between would have more than made up for it, as this was the unlikely genesis of one of London's most remarkable and pioneering law enforcement bodies: the Women's Police Volunteers.

MARGARET DAMER DAWSON
(1873–1920)
By the outbreak of war in 1914, the house on Cheyne Row was home to an all-round Renaissance Woman, Margaret Damer Dawson. Dawson was a well-connected woman of independent means, a Royal Academy-trained musician, an experienced Alpine mountaineer, a keen motorist and one of the country's earliest anti-vivisectionists. She was also a passionate feminist whose experiences fighting for

women's suffrage impressed upon her the need for change of a different order: a women's police force.

Those who knew Dawson lauded her fearlessness. Her work in animal rights took her into slaughterhouses across England, for instance; not the first place you'd expect to find an Edwardian lady of means. Her partner in life, love and work, Mary Allen, would later say of Dawson, 'Danger steeled her; she was encouraged, even inspired by difficulties.'[16]

In part, Dawson and the other fearless women she gathered around her were motivated by their shared experiences as suffragettes at the hands of an exclusively male police force. Added to this, the influx of Belgian refugees into London at the start of the First World War opened her eyes to another phenomenon: the spread and stealth of the British sex industry. Too many of the Belgian women and girls Dawson encountered, all entirely uprooted and without resource, were helpless to fend off the advances of pimps.

The war brought with it worries of another new threat to the women of Britain. In 1914, the Defence of the Realm Act, known colloquially as 'DORA', gave Parliament sweeping powers for the duration of the war, not least over civilian behaviour. In areas close to army barracks, for instance, local women (though generally not men), were subjected to a tight curfew, intended to discourage nocturnal relations with men in uniform. What women like Margaret Dawson and Mary Allen feared most, however, was that wartime promiscuity might also result in a return to the days of the 1860 Contagious Disease Act, when women were routinely hauled off the streets of London and forced to undergo an internal examination in a misguided attempt to stem the spread of STIs in the capital.

As the summer of 1914 came to an end, Dawson was more convinced than ever that to stand any lasting hope of social and political equality, women needed protecting, both from the predatory advances of men, and from what she perceived to be their own folly. Dawson was not alone in her conviction that the country needed women in

---

[16] Allen, Mary Sophia, *The Pioneer Policewoman* (Chatto & Windus, 1925).

the police force, but she was in a stronger position than most to exert influence: she had an elevated social background and, almost exceptionally among her fellow suffragists, a clean record. Better yet, she was a personal friend of Sir Edward Henry, Commissioner of London's Metropolitan Police Force.

So it was that by August of 1914 a gathering of mature women (the youngest among them was already thirty-six), all of them well-educated, privileged women of means, most of them suffragettes, gathered at 10 Cheyne Row to set out their strategies for the establishment of the country's first all-women police force, the Women's Police Volunteers. Sir Edward Henry granted them permission to patrol the streets, with a particular focus on enforcing those aspects of DORA pertaining to prostitution, and gave them a degree of recognition in the form of official ID cards.

Initially Dawson didn't assume leadership of the WPV; that role was taken on by Nina Boyle. But she designed the uniform, something she regarded as essential if they were to be taken seriously on the streets. The uniform was in almost every respect the same as that worn by male police officers of the day; it made almost no concession to femininity. After the WVP took delivery of a number of motorcycles in 1917, the women of the WVP cast off their long skirts in favour of trousers, scandalous in any other context. Dawson embraced the uniform, cropping her hair short and wearing nothing else until her death in 1920. Mary Allen similarly embraced the liberation from restrictive women's clothing given by the uniform; she finished the look off with a similarly cropped hairstyle and a monocle. Early recruits were trained in first aid, criminal law, police court procedure and jiu jitsu, working from rooms at Scotland Yard's former headquarters at St Stephen's House, Westminster.

Dawson's vision of the WPV was unwavering: she saw its sights set firmly on the fight against promiscuity. In the autumn of 1914 they were called upon to serve the population of Grantham in Lincolnshire, the site of a twenty thousand-man military base which was causing some consternation locally. Using the powers enabled by DORA, Grantham imposed a 6 p.m. to 7 a.m. curfew on local prostitutes, which Mary Allen and her colleague, Ellen Harburn, were called upon to enforce. They did so with gusto and with Dawson's impassioned support.

Nina Boyle, however, was horrified: what troubled her most was that policing the curfew called upon Allen and Harburn not to apply the strict letter of the law, but to *interpret* the morality of any women they encountered in Grantham. In practice, this meant that they entered private homes, raided billets and hostels and expelled hundreds of women whom they *suspected* of immorality. This was not the strict policing of female criminality Boyle had envisaged, but when she challenged Dawson, she quickly discovered hers was a lone voice. Almost to a woman, the WPV stood with Dawson, who rose to lead a new version of the organisation, renamed the Women's Police Service. The experience of the Volunteers in Grantham made a lasting impact: in 1915, the local constabulary appointed Edith Smith the first woman police officer with the power of arrest in English history.

When peace came, Dawson campaigned hard for her volunteers to be taken on by the Metropolitan Police, but her efforts to sustain the Women's Police Service as an integral entity within the Metropolitan Police would ultimately prove unsuccessful. The British establishment nurtured several reservations: too many of the women within the WPS had been militant suffragettes, but malaise too stemmed from their sexuality and the fact that many of them were highly educated. WPCs who were brighter than their male colleagues was not a scenario Scotland Yard was yet ready to embrace. Significantly, however, Commissioner Henry's successor, Nevil Macready, criticised the Women's Police Service's heavy-handed treatment of prostitutes, without a similar reciprocal treatment of their male clients. Consequently, in 1918, when Macready established London's Metropolitan Women Police Patrols in 1918, Dawson's WPS was not among its number. Only one of the original Volunteers, Mary Allen's sister, Margaret 'Dolly' Hampton, would continue to serve as a police officer within the Met.

Dawson and Allen were rewarded for their pivotal role in

establishing a need for uniformed women police officers when they were awarded OBEs in 1918. Two years later, Dawson died suddenly of a heart attack, a month before her twenty-eighth birthday, leaving her entire estate to Mary Allen. The seeds of change had been sown, however. Dawson lived long enough to see women granted the vote. And though neither she nor Mary Allen ever wore the Metropolitan Police uniform, twenty-five other women did so from 1918; by 1923, three years after Dawson's death, WPCs within the Met were finally given the power of arrest.

11 KENSINGTON SQUARE, KENSINGTON

At the end of the nineteenth century, Kensington Square with its gated garden was home to an eclectic mix of city folk, artists and actors. Famously, Isadora Duncan (see also page 55) and her brother Raymond, who lodged for a time on the square, were spotted dancing in the gardens at dusk one evening in the late summer of 1899. Fortuitously, they were observed by a very well-connected neighbour, one of London's most celebrated actresses of the era, Mrs Patrick Campbell, known affectionately as 'Mrs Pat'. Indeed Mrs Pat was so taken with Isadora, she introduced her to London's social elite, entirely changing the young dancer's fortunes.

Whether the stockbroker and his family living at number 11 spotted their strange American neighbours striking Pre-Raphaelite poses and writhing in loose Grecian costume in the setting sun that evening isn't recorded. Perhaps they were too preoccupied with their young children, the youngest of whom was a daughter, barely two years old in 1899, who would develop a fabulously idiosyncratic occupation of her own, leading her to a pioneering and much-publicised career.

JOAN BEAUCHAMP PROCTER

(1897–1931)

By the age of ten, Joan Procter was a sickly child, troubled with debilitating and uncomfortable digestive issues; but though her health impacted on her attendance at school, it did nothing to curb her insatiable curiosity. From an early age, she and her sister, Christabel, were fascinated with botany and naturalism. By the time she was ten Joan had honed her interest to amphibian and reptilian life and began an impressive collection of pet lizards and snakes. Dinner time at the Procters' home would have been an alarming affair for visitors, with Joan's much-favoured Dalmatian lizard a constant companion, even at the table. By the age of sixteen, she had added a small crocodile to her menagerie and was prone to taking it with her to school.

With her health precluding a Cambridge degree, at eighteen Procter was taken on by Belgian zoologist, George Boulenger, keeper of reptiles and fish at London's Natural History museum. Under his guidance, she furthered her study of zoology and began to publish a number of well-received scientific papers, the first of which examined pit vipers, when she was still only nineteen years old. A year later, she was made a fellow of the Zoological Society and three years after that, she took over from Boulenger at the museum, cataloguing and describing animals donated to the collection and gaining recognition for the calibre of her work. But it was her artistic flair, as well as her vast body of knowledge on the subject, which first brought Procter to the attention of the Boulengers' son, Edward.

Impressed by the accuracy and artistry of the models and paintings she produced for display at the museum, Edward invited Procter to collaborate on a project at London Zoo, designing a new aquarium. The six-month project in 1923 was a huge success and when Edward was made director of the aquarium later that year, Joan stepped up as curator of the reptile house, the first woman ever to have done so.

The press fell instantly in love with the elfin young woman with a love of all things reptilian. Her appointment was covered on both sides of the Atlantic, such was the draw of her story. The 'Zoo Girl Snake Expert', as one 1923 by-line declared her, was soon proving herself to be a significant asset, both to the Zoo's takings at the gate and to the body of scientific understanding on the care of captive reptiles. Procter developed an expertise in handling the animals, even standing down an escaped bear on one occasion and trapping it in a toilet cubicle. She built a remarkable rapport with the reptiles in her care and in so doing, identified a number of previously unknown diseases and displayed a competence in carrying out a number of pioneering veterinary procedures. She continued her design work, constructing the enormously popular Monkey Hill for the baboons in 1924 and more significantly, designing a new Reptile House in 1926, the world's first purpose-built construction for captive reptiles. Procter pioneered the use of specialist glass which enabled the reptiles to be bathed in natural ultraviolet light, one of her many other design and technological features which were subsequently taken up in reptile houses at other zoos. She was even the brains behind the design of the Zoo's iconic roofed entrance gates, flanked on either side by neat white gate towers and porthole windows.

Meanwhile Procter's academic work continued to garner widespread accolades earning her an honorary doctorate from the University of Cambridge in 1931. She demonstrated to a stunned scientific community that Komodo dragons could be trained to behave entirely differently in captivity from their typical predatory nature in the wild, taming one so completely, it displayed affectionate behaviour towards her and she frequently led it around the Zoo on a leash, allowing visitors to interact with it.

As her health began to fail, Joan's capacity to work at the Zoo became increasingly impaired. By now, she had moved to live nearby in St Mark's Square, with a pet chimpanzee and several venomous snakes and lizards, and was often to be seen moving through the grounds of the Zoo in an electric wheelchair, her three-foot Komodo dragon trailing alongside on its leash. When she died after a long battle with cancer at the age of just thirty-four, her death was mourned on both sides of the Atlantic. Obituaries lauded her expertise, her extensive scientific output, her work at the London Zoo and her design work. They mentioned too her lifelong battle with her health. Her close friend and colleague, Edward Boulenger, summed up his feelings about Procter in an obituary for *Nature* magazine a month after her death: 'Seldom has the triumph of force of mind over physical weakness been more vividly illustrated than in the case of Dr. Joan Beauchamp Procter'.

Procter's legacy extended beyond London Zoo; her outstanding work in the field of herpetology and her pioneering practice in the design of enclosures and habitats for captive zoo animals had lasting and widespread impact. The fact of her quick rise to prominence within the field and the respect she garnered from her peers, in spite of her presence as a sole woman in a male domain, makes her achievement all the more remarkable.

4 CADOGAN LANE, BELGRAVIA

The northern end of Cadogan Lane is a tiny cul-de-sac of mews homes, originally built as stabling and coach houses for the large properties on Cadogan Lane. The lane is cut through by Pont Street, with its bars, restaurants and shops in the heart of Belgravia. The entire area forms part of Belgravia's Hans Conservation area, so-named after Hans Sloane, on whose estate the region was built. By the 1960s this region of Chelsea was the beating heart of 'Swinging' London but for three months in 1969, the unremarkable mews house at number 4 Cadogan Lane, nestled in its quiet cul-de-sac, was the last home of one of the most iconic movie stars of the twentieth century.

JUDY GARLAND
(1922–69)

In March 1969, days after her fifth wedding to London nightclub owner, Mickey Deans, 47-year-old Judy Garland spoke to the British press. They were preoccupied by the poor attendance at her wedding, where only fifty of the several-hundred-strong guest list attended. The no-shows included some of the biggest names of the day, including Eva Gabor, John Gielgud, James Mason, Bette Davis and Albert Finney. Clive Hirschhorn, chief profile writer for the *Sunday Express* in 1969, ran with the headline, 'Judy Weds But Stars Stay Away'. Garland wouldn't be drawn and instead wanted to celebrate a feeling that had eluded her for her entire life: contentment. In part, she attributed her sense of well-being to the city itself, telling the *Daily Express*,

'I don't know if London still needs me, but I certainly need it! It's good and kind to me. I feel at home here. The people understand me and I'm not aware of the cruelty I've so often felt in the States.'

Three months later, Garland's new husband discovered her dead in the bathroom of their little mews home, having taken an accidental overdose of the sedatives on which she had been dependent for decades.

Judy Garland's legacy was indisputably one of the finest in Hollywood history. Signed by MGM at the age of sixteen, she had graced the big screen for three decades and is remembered for some of the best-loved songs of the century, including her two signature ballads, 'Somewhere Over The Rainbow' from *The Wizard of Oz* at the start of her career, and 'The Man That Got Away', from the remarkable *A Star is Born* in 1954.

Scratch through the Hollywood veneer and it's clear to see the cruelty she wanted to leave behind. Her obituary in *The New York Times* on 23 June 1969 makes clear that fame came at great personal cost. In her teens, Hollywood producer and executive Louis B. Mayer called her, 'that fat kid' and, 'my little hunchback',[17] and she claimed that the studios insisted she take Benzedrine, an amphetamine regarded then as something of a wonderdrug, as a means of keeping her energy high and her weight down. 'They'd give us pep pills. Then they'd take us to the studio hospital and knock us cold with sleeping pills . . . after four hours they'd wake us up and give us the pep pills again . . .'[18] By the age of eighteen, he had signed her up for $150,000 a picture, as well as weekly sessions with a psychiatrist.

[17] Clive Hirschhorn, former chief profile writer with the *Sunday Express*, told the *New York Post* on 4 April 2012 that he met Garland backstage during her five-week run at Talk of the Town in 1969. Hirschhorn recalled, 'She talked about how MGM had hooked her and Mickey Rooney on drugs to keep them awake during filming, and she told me that Louis B. Mayer . . . called her 'my little hunchback'.

[18] *The New York Times*, 23 June 1969.

She later recalled, 'No wonder I was strange. Imagine whipping out of bed, dashing over to the doctor's office, lying down on a torn leather couch, telling my troubles to an old man who couldn't hear, who answered with an accent I couldn't understand, and then dashing to Metro to make movie love to Mickey Rooney.'[19] When the amphetamines kept her from sleeping, she would be sent to medics for sleeping pills and tranquillisers. And when the sleeping pills stopped her from being up and ready for work, she was given more uppers. It was a cycle she would battle throughout her life.

The cruelty persisted: for the next twenty years or more, the press pored over her four failed marriages, her mounting debts, her fluctuating weight, her many hospital stays, her sacking from several movie sets. Behind the scenes, there were several suicide attempts and an ongoing battle with drug and alcohol addiction. In the face of so many challenges, her resilience seems remarkable: she bounced back from each knockback, constantly returning to the stage or screen, making new records, more movies, winning more awards. At the age of thirty-nine, she became the youngest actor ever to have been awarded the Cecil B. DeMille Lifetime Achievement Award.

By her mid-forties, however, her stamina was failing along with her health. Her final role in 1967 was to have been in the big screen adaptation of Jacqueline Susann's novel, *Valley of the Dolls*, playing Neely O'Hara, a character Susann had based on Garland; but she was fired when she persistently failed to show up to rehearsals. In what seems almost prophetically tragic, the 'dolls' of the title were street slang for Seconal, the very sedative which would claim Garland's life on the floor of a Chelsea bathroom in June 1969.

Upon her death, Garland weighed just seventy pounds. She left $4 million in debts; her funeral expenses were picked up by her close friend, Frank Sinatra, with whom she had an affair in the 1950s. The untimely death of one of the most loved voices of the century was covered by *The New York Times* with an opening line which referred to 'the pathos of her personal life' and detailed her

---

[19] *The New York Times*, 23 June 1969.

'fruitless search for happiness' even before it honoured her 'extraordinary talent'.

Number 4 Cadogan Lane was perhaps an overly modest final
home for a multi-award winning Hollywood legend. But to Garland,
this little corner of Belgravia was a final brief taste of the quiet compassion for which she had been grasping since adolescence, and for
the briefest of moments, she had felt contentment and gratitude.

A life lived large and a final scene worthy of commemoration.

9 Upper Phillimore Gardens, Chelsea

Emilia Jessie Boucherett
(1825–1905)
Descended from Lincolnshire landed gentry, Emilia Jessie Boucherett
was a leading British feminist activist and journalist who worked with
the Langham Place Group on the most contentious feminist issues of
the day. She campaigned extensively in support of the passage of the
Married Women's Property Act of 1870 and was central to the launch of
the campaign for women's suffrage in London, decades before women
were finally enfranchised in Britain in 1919. Boucherett founded
The Society for Promoting the Employment of Women, edited *The
Englishwoman's Review* and later, *The Women's Suffrage Journal*. She
lived at Upper Phillimore Gardens with her sister and a domestic staff
of six.

12 Abingdon Mansions, Abingdon Road, Kensington

Rebecca Clarke
(1886–1979)
Rebecca Clarke was a pioneering string player, trained in violin and
viola at the Royal Academy of Music and one of the first women to
have studied composition at the Royal College of Music. She moved in
as a boarder at Abingdon Mansions in 1910, after her father threw her
out of his home following her criticism of his adultery, forcing her to

leave the Royal College and support herself. At this point she became a professional musician, taken on by Sir Henry Wood along with five other women to play in the Queen's Orchestra, one of the first women ever to be accepted to play with a professional orchestra. She moved to the US to further her career in 1916 and her reputation grew; by the 1920s she embarked upon a solo career and a world tour. Her musical career was scuppered by the outbreak of the Second World War, which left her stranded in the US without a visa to return to the UK. She took work as a governess in order to support herself but continued to compose, writing nearly a hundred works during her lifetime, much of which have been revived since the 1970s.

17 LANSDOWNE ROAD, HOLLAND PARK

MADAME BLAVATSKY
(1831–91)

Yelena Petrovna Blavatsky arrived in London in 1885, having travelled extensively across Europe, North America and India, leaving a trail as laden with devotees as it was controversy. Born in the Ukraine into an aristocratic family, her stay in London marked the last four years of an eventful life. She had uncovered a unique psychic power, she claimed, while studying with a group of enlightened beings whom she called the 'Masters of the Ancient Wisdom'.

In New York in the 1870s, she had joined forces with some of the leading proponents of the burgeoning spiritualist movement, which had gained enormous popularity on both sides of the Atlantic since the 1850s. Blavatsky had introduced herself as a guru and a medium and was convincing enough to have attracted a significant public following. By 1875, she honed her beliefs and her public persona, establishing the Theosophical Society, publishing a series of books which attracted a remarkable, global audience. Branches of the Theosophical Society sprang up around the world, including, in 1885, in London. Two years later, Madame Blavatsky moved to 17 Lansdowne Road, home to leading theosophist, Bertram Keightley, and transformed the house into the 'Blavatsky Lodge', the largest theosophist meeting house in the UK. She remained there until the year before her death in 1891.

Blavatsky was a charismatic figure and her philosophical and spiritual beliefs and practices were not without vociferous critics, but she had another significant talent: she was a gifted self-publicist, a woman of enormous charisma and personality; a one-woman phenomenon with a global reach and cross-cultural influence. She was central to the late nineteenth-century spread of Hindu and Buddhist tenets across the West, as well as the exponential rise of occultism, spiritualism and paranormalism in Victorian Britain, which would draw in the likes of Queen Victoria, Prince Albert and Sir Arthur Conan Doyle.

CHAPTER TWELVE

Hammersmith & Fulham

4 FAIRHOLME ROAD, FULHAM

EVELYN CHEESMAN
(1881–1969)

In 1901, 19-year-old Evelyn Cheesman embarked on adulthood in an unremarkable way, as a governess to the children of a retired army captain at 4 Fairholme Road, Fulham. Life as a governess, however, was never going to contain Cheesman's adventurous spirit or enquiring mind and after the First World War she took an altogether different path. Unable to study veterinary medicine because of a gender bar, she turned her attention instead to entomology. By 1920, she had become the first woman ever appointed as curator of the Insect House at London Zoo. She proved a voracious entomologist, undertaking eight expeditions around the South Pacific during her lifetime, including becoming the first woman ever to have done so solo, surviving disease and starvation, navigating all manner of hazards and undertaking systematic investigations of South Pacific Island insects.

Disillusioned with the poor organisation of her first expedition, Cheesman broke off from the party and continued alone, undertaking the next seven expeditions largely solo. She had four species of South Pacific tree frog named after her, discovered a new variety of orchid, the spectacular blue *Dendrobium azureum*, and during the course of her career, donated seventy thousand insect species to the Natural History Museum in London. She made her final expedition to the South Pacific at the age of seventy-three, following a hip replacement operation.

CHAPTER THIRTEEN

Richmond upon Thames

LADY MARY WORTLEY MONTAGU

(1689–1762)

Lady Mary Wortley Montagu was a charismatic and vivacious woman with an empathetic, resilient personality. As a young woman, she defied her father's wish that she marry Irishman Clotworthy Skeffington by eloping with lawyer and MP, Sir Edward Wortley Montagu, British Ambassador to the Ottoman Empire in Turkey.

Mary travelled to Turkey with her husband, although the marriage was increasingly strained. She wrote extensively of her travels through the Middle East, showing a great affection and respect for the people, culture and traditions she encountered there and condemning what she came to see had been a significant misrepresentation of the religion of Islam by previous British travellers. Back in London, she edited her *Embassy Letters,* but decided against their publication; they were published posthumously in 1837 by her granddaughter, Lady Louisa Stuart, to great European acclaim, making her the first woman to have published a travel journal of the Middle East.

An ardent feminist, Mary Wortley Montagu published a series of essays challenging gender restrictions on education and opportunity; and after learning of the smallpox while in Turkey, she had her own two children, Edward and Mary, inoculated and became a leading advocate of a vaccination programme against the disease in England.

In 1717, she was introduced to leading poet, Alexander Pope, who became infatuated with her and pursued her for several years. Although her letters to Pope suggest she certainly didn't return his affections, her marriage with Wortley Montagu grew more distant and the two eventually went their separate ways. By 1727, for reasons now obscured by time, relations between Pope and Lady Montagu soured and the English poet published a poem satirising her spitefully, to which she responded in kind, triggering a highly public poetical sparring match, which the pair sustained for a decade. She left England for Europe in 1736, having fallen in love with an Italian count named Francesco Algarotti; though the affair was short-lived, she lived happily on the Continent until hearing of the death of Wortley Montagu in 1761, whereupon she returned to London. During her homeward journey, she handed her *Embassy Letters* to a clergyman in Rotterdam for safekeeping. She died in London seven months after her return.

CHAPTER FOURTEEN

Hillingdon

MOORCROFT HOUSE, NOW MOORCROFT PARK, HARLINGTON ROAD

LOUISA NOTTIDGE

(1802–58)

Louisa Nottidge lived a quiet childhood, raised within a family who were strictly devoted to Bible studies in their large home in Essex. But after the death of her father, Louisa and her four sisters were persuaded to part with their considerable inheritance by a de-frocked Anglican minister named Henry James Prince.

Prince was as charismatic as he was controversial and by preying on vulnerable, unmarried or widowed women of independent means, he had succeeded in becoming the unlikely leader of a remarkable religious cult called the Agapemonites, with a large estate in Spaxton in Somerset he called *Agapemone*, The Abode of Love. Three of the Nottidge sisters were hurriedly married into the cult to tie them in, but before Louisa could be similarly wedded in, she was removed from Spaxton under the cover of darkness, entirely against her wishes, by three of her male relatives. In an effort to constrain her and prevent her return, Louisa's brother, brother-in-law and cousin had her incarcerated at the Moorcroft House Lunatic Asylum in Hillingdon on the grounds of 'religious mania'. They would ultimately fail in their mission: Louisa escaped and returned to The Abode of Love, where she lived out the rest of her days. But she fought back against her brother, cousin and brother-in-law, successfully suing them for false imprisonment and abduction. The case attracted massive attention, covered at length daily by the national press and throwing up a highly contentious public debate about the endemic spread of the enforced incarceration of women by their male relatives in British lunatic asylums.

121 STATION ROAD (NOW RAZED), WEST DRAYTON

In the early years of the 1930s, Station Road, West Drayton, was lined by a number of large, three-storey, double-bay-fronted Victorian villas, with a pub at number 125, The Six Bells, which dated back to 1826. In the 1930s, West Drayton still retained the air of a village, before the urgent need for new housing in the post-war period saw the area become increasingly urbanised. By 1934, the new family who moved into the generously proportioned house at number 121 were untypical of the era in lifestyle, philosophy and political beliefs and were especially noteworthy for their combined contribution to science.

KATHLEEN LONSDALE
(1903–71)

There was nothing auspicious about the early years in the life of Kathleen Lonsdale. The youngest of ten children, she was born into poverty in County Kildare, to a diminutive but formidable mother of London-Scottish descent and a father who, although hard working, grew increasingly ailing and driven to drink. Her father may well have felt affection towards his family, Lonsdale later pondered, but it was neither evident nor especially reciprocated.

With Irish instability mounting, Lonsdale and her siblings moved with their mother to South East England during her childhood. At school she excelled and was granted a scholarship to study at the County Grammar, becoming the only girl to attend the boys' school in order to study the sciences, which were not otherwise made available to girls of the day. At sixteen, she earned a place at London University's Bedford College to study mathematics, quickly switching to physics and graduating top of her year. Her academic gift was to set her on a course for a remarkable lifetime of scientific research and groundbreaking firsts.

From the start to the end of her career, Lonsdale made a series of important advances in the science of crystallography, and was a pioneer in the field of X-ray diffraction, as well as pursuing such a broad range of scientific investigations that the authors of her obituaries struggled to give her work full credit in limited column inches. Her former colleague, Dorothy M. C. Hodgkin, credited Lonsdale with an immense body of work, which in addition to significant scientific discoveries and advances, included what she described as immeasurable 'small, interesting comments' which 'defy classification'. Hodgkin noted, for instance, that Lonsdale had trialled the first use of the X-ray microscope developed by W. L. Bragg and Charles Bunn, using it to complete a vital element of the work which preceded the definition of the structure of penicillin.

Within her field, Lonsdale's prowess was widely recognised, earning her a remarkable list of honours. In 1944, she was one of two women who were formally nominated to become members of the Royal Society – the first to have been granted membership in the Society's history (the Society's statutes had to be altered in order to enable their election). In 1949, Lonsdale was the first woman to become a tenured professor at University College, London when she was made professor of chemistry and head of crystallography. By 1956, not only had she been made a Dame for her Services to Science, but she had also become the first woman to have been appointed president of the International Union of Crystallography. In 1968, she was the first woman to hold the office of president of the British Association for the Advancement of Science.

But her marriage to fellow scientist and academic Thomas Jackson Lonsdale in 1927 had briefly presented itself as something of a conundrum for her: should she now abandon her work and instead focus on keeping house and having a family? In an extraordinarily avant-garde move, Thomas wouldn't hear of it, insisting he hadn't married her for 'free housekeeping'. They shared domestic duties, shopping together for groceries, for instance. Later, when Lonsdale had three small children and had been maintaining her research from home in order to combine work with motherhood, her absence at the Royal Institute was so keenly felt that senior colleagues awarded her an annual grant of £300 with which to finance alternative domestic arrangements so as to enable her to return.

These were exceedingly enlightened gestures for the era and stand as a measure of quite how important her scientific research was considered to be.

Lonsdale's remarkable achievements extended beyond the laboratory, however. Raised a Baptist, she and her husband spent the early years of their marriage searching for a branch of Christianity that sat more comfortably with their scientific bent. They found it in the Quaker movement, strengthening Lonsdale's pre-existing pacifist convictions, which had initially been formed during the First World War. When war broke out again in 1939, Lonsdale was exempt from all but civil defence duties because of the age of her children; participation of this kind, however, sat too uncomfortably with her and she resisted. When she then refused to pay a fine of £2 for non-registration, a frustrated magistrate sentenced her to a month at HM Prison Holloway.

Typically, Lonsdale made impressive use of her time behind bars, forming a lasting relationship with the prison visiting service and devoting lifelong energy into campaigning to improve conditions for prison inmates. In fact, she brought vigour and passion to everything that mattered to her. A devoted wife and mother, an important and widely lauded pioneer in the science of crystallography, she was also a tireless pacifist, converting the top floor of their home on Station Road into a self-contained apartment and giving it over to German refugee families in the inter-war years. It was no surprise, then, that after the atomic bomb was used to end the Second World War, Lonsdale also threw herself into the international pacifist movement, talking extensively abroad and publishing widely on the subject. She became vice-president of the British Atomic Scientists' Association and in 1957, disheartened by global politics, in three furious weeks she wrote her Penguin Special, *Is Peace Possible?*

In an era where schoolgirls were uniformly prevented from studying science and female graduates barred from attaining full membership of many leading universities, Kathleen Lonsdale achieved the unthinkable. She established herself as one of the nation's most groundbreaking and significant chemists and set a precedent for enabling mothers to return to work. Lonsdale's former home on Station Road may be gone, but her remarkable legacy is lasting and far-reaching.

Appendix

By 1902, Ethel Smyth's works included:

We Watched Her Breathing Through the Night (1876), part-song by
    Thomas Hood.

String Quartet No. 1 in A minor (1878), one movement.

String Quartet in D minor (1880).

Trio for violin, cello and piano in D minor (1880).

Sonata for cello and piano in C minor (1880).

String Quintet in B minor (1882–84), two movements.

Five Sacred Part-Songs Based on Chorale Tunes (1882–84).

String Quartet in E flat (1882–84).

String Quintet in E, Op. 1 (1883).

String Trio in D (1887).

String Quartet in C minor (1883).

String Quartet in C (1886–88).

Sonata for cello and piano in A minor, Op. 5 (1887).

Sonata for violin and piano in A minor, Op. 7 (1887).

Sonata No. 1 in C (1877).

Sonata No. 2 (*Geistinger*) in C-sharp minor (1877).

Sonata No. 3 in D (1877), two movements.

Aus der Jugenzeit!! in E minor (1877–80).

Four-part Dances (1877–80).

Two-part Invention in D (1877–80).

Two-part Suite in E (1877–80).

Variations on an Original Theme (of an Exceedingly Dismal Nature)
    in D flat (1878).

Prelude and Fugue in C (1878–84).

Prelude and Fugue in F sharp (1880).

Fugue à 5 (1882–84).

Short Chorale Preludes (1882–84).

Study on 'O wie selig seid ihr doch, ihr Frommen' (1882–84).

Prelude and Fugue for Thin People (*c.* 1883).

Lieder und Balladen with piano, Op. 3 (*c.* 1877).

Lieder with piano, Op. 4 (*c.* 1877).

Eight songs (*c.* 1877).

Nine Rounds (1878–84).

The Song of Love, Op. 8 (1888), cantata by Smyth after *The Song of Songs*.

Overture to Shakespeare's Antony and Cleopatra (1889) (18 October 1890, The Crystal Palace, London).

Serenade in D (1889) (26 April 1890, The Crystal Palace, London).

Suite for Piano Four Hands (published 1891), rearrangement of Suite for Strings, Op. 1A.

Mass in D (1891) (18 January 1893, Royal Albert Hall, London).

Suite for Strings, Op. 1A (published 1891), rearrangement from String Quintet in E, Op. 1.

Fantastio (1892–94), comic opera in two acts by Henry Bennet Brewster and Smyth after Alfred de Musset (24 May 1898, Hoftheater, Weimar).

Wedding Anthem for choir and organ (*c.* 1900).

Der Wald (1899–1901), opera in one act by Henry Brewster and Smyth (9 April 1902, Königliches Opernhaus, Berlin).

Bibliography

Extensive use has been made of primary sources during the research process of this book. Ancestry has been an invaluable source for electoral registers, census returns, telephone directories, Atlantic crossing passenger lists, slave registers and inventories, military archives and parish registers. Many of the stories could not have been written without access to online newspaper archives, the British Library Newspaper archive in particular. I have been hugely enabled by University College London's online database, Legacies of British slave-ownership, a meticulous and extensive resource documenting slave ownership. The researching of the homes and streets which appear in the book has been enabled by British History Online, with its extensive collection of source material, not least of which are the surveys of London, undertaken and published in 1720, the 1890s and in 1913. The book has also drawn upon a number of additional documents pertaining to individual women, stored at the British Library, the National Archives and the London Metropolitan Archives.

Individual stories and addresses have been brought into sharper focus by a variety of secondary sources, biographies and histories.

Atkinson, Diane, *The Criminal Conversation of Mrs Norton* (Random House, 2013).

Bamgbose, Kemi, 'Sarah Forbes Bonetta: The Yoruba Princess who Captured Queen Victoria's Heart' (*New African Woman*, 24 November 2016).

Bell, Gertrude, *Persian Pictures* (Anthem Press, 2005).

Berger, Marilyn, 'Jessica Tandy, a Patrician Star of Theater and Film' (*The New York Times*, 12 September 1994).

Bret, David, *George Formby: An Intimate Biography of the Troubled Genius* (Lulu Press, 2014).

British Library Untold Lives Blog, Margaret Makepeace: 'Whatever happened to Eliza Armstrong?' (16 April 2012).

Brook, Claire, *British Women Surgeons and their Patients, 1860–1918* (Cambridge University Press, 2017).

Buchan, James, 'Miss Bell's Lines in the Sand' (*Guardian*, 12 March 2003).

Burness, Edwina and Jerry Griswold, 'P. L. Travers, The Art of Fiction No. 63' (*The Paris Review*, issue 86, Winter 1982).

Canel, Annie and Ruth Oldenziel, *Crossing Boundaries, Building Bridges* (Routledge, 2005).

Chadburn, Maud, 'Appreciations: Miss M.M. Chadburn', appended to 'Obituary', *British Medical Journal*, 9 January 1926.

Cobbold, Evelyn, *Pilgrimage to Mecca* (Arabian Publishing, 2009).

Cutpurse, Moll, author, and Randall S. Nakayama, ed., *The life and death of Mrs. Mary Frith: commonly called Moll Cutpurse*, 1662 with a facsimile of the original edition (Garland, 1993).

Davies, Andrew John, 'Site Unseen – Admiral's House, Hampstead' (*Independent*, 11 September 1995).

Durham, Mary Edith, *The Sarajevo Crime* (G. Allen & Unwin, 1925).

Ferguson, Moira, ed., *The History of Mary Prince, A West Indian Slave, Related By Herself* (University of Michigan Press, 1987).

Fraser, Robert, *Night Thoughts* (OUP, 2012).

Freeman, Colin, 'How Gertrude Bell Caused a Desert Storm' (*Telegraph*, 12 July 2006).

Harrison, Barbara, *Not Only the 'Dangerous Trades': Women's Work and Health in Britain, 1880–1914* (Taylor & Francis, 1996).

Hodgkin, Dorothy M. C., 'Biographical Memoirs – Kathleen Lonsdale 28 January 1903–1 April 1971' (Royal Society Publishing.org, 1 November 1975).

Izbicki, John, 'Dorothy Lawrence: The Man That Never Was' (*Independent*, 11 November 1999).

Leigh-Smith Bodichon, Barbara, 'A Brief Summary in Plain Language of the Most Important Laws Concerning Women, Together with a Few Observations Thereon' (J. Chapman, London, 1954, reprinted in Susan Groag Bell and Karen M. Offen, eds., *Women, the Family, and Freedom: the Debate in Documents*, Volume I, 1750–1880 (Stanford University Press, 1983).

Lewis, Roger, 'A Stratford Stalin' (*The Spectator*, 8 November 2014).

Lind af Hageby, Lizzie and Leisa Schartau, *The Shambles of Science: Extracts from the Diary of Two Students of Physiology* (E. Bell, 1903).

––, *The Shambles of Science: Extracts from the Diary of Two Students of Physiology* (Scholar's Choice, 2015).

Mackirdy, Olive Christian Malvery, *The Soul Market* (Hutchinson & Co., 1907).

Mackirdy, Archibald, Mrs, and W. N. Willis, *The White Slave Market* (Stanley Paul & Co., 1912).

Marshik, Celia, *British Modernism and Censorship* (Cambridge University Press, 2006).

Montagu, Lady Mary Wortley, author, and Anita Desai, introduction, *The Turkish Embassy Letters* (Virago, 1994).

Picardie, Justine, 'Was P L Travers the Real Mary Poppins?' (*Telegraph*, 28 October 2008).

Ross, Ellen, ed., *Slum Travelers: Ladies and London Poverty, 1860–1920* (University of California Press, 2007).

Russell, John, 'In 1936, Surrealism Ruled the Creative Roost' (*The New York Times*, 30 March 1988).

Shipman, David, 'Obituary – Jessica Tandy' (*Independent*, 12 September 1994).

Sternlicht, Sanford V., *A Reader's Guide to Modern British Drama* (Syracuse Press, 2004).

Theatre Workshop, *Oh! What a Lovely War* (Bloomsbury, 2014).

Wajid, Sara, 'They bought me as a butcher would a calf or a lamb' (*Guardian*, 19 October 2007).

Wharncliffe, Lord and W. Moy Thomas, ed., *Letters and Works of Lady Mary Wortley Montagu* (Henry G. Bohn, 1861).

Wheatley, Phillis, *Poems on Various Subjects, Religious and Moral* (A. Bell, 1773) (Available in full at www.bartleby.com).

––, Phillis Wheatley: *Complete Writings* (Penguin, 2001).

––, *Poems of Phillis Wheatley, a Native African and a Slave* (Read, 2008).

White, Caroline Alice, *Sweet Hampstead and its Associations* (1900) (Kessinger, 2009).

Wroath, Joan, *Until They Are Seven: The Origins of Women's Legal Rights* (Waterside Press, 1989).

Index

Note: page numbers in **bold** refer to map entries.

A WOMAN LIVED HERE

University College, London 159
Upper Phillimore Gardens, Chelsea 149

vaccinations 155
Victoria, Queen 73, 80, 81–2, 102, 151
vivisection 74–5, 139
Voices (literary radio show) 19
Voltaire 15

Walworth 19–20
Walworth Road 19–20
War Office 46
Warnock Report 1978 72
Warwick Square, Pimlico 54–7
Washington, George 12, 15, 33
Watch With Mother (TV show) 129
Watts, George Frederick 66
waxworks 31, 32–4
Wedgwood, Josiah 62
Welchman, Gordon 25
Wellington, Duke of 65, 116
West Drayton 158–61
West Norwood 24–6
West Sussex County Asylum 74
Westbrook, Harriet 62
Westminster 28, 29–76
Westminster Abbey museum 32
Wheatley, John 10–12, 13
Wheatley, Mary 11
Wheatley, Nathaniel 10, 11, 12, 13
Wheatley, Phillis 4, 10–15
    Poems on Subjects Religious and Moral (1773)
      13–14
Wheatley, Susanna 10, 13
Whigs 57, 59
White, Caroline 95
Whitley Council Committee 88
Widdowson, Elsie 4, 20
Wilde, Oscar 62
Williams, Tennessee 123

A Streetcar Named Desire (1947) 123
Wilson, Harriette 65
Windsor, Barbara 23
Winsloe, Christa 122
wireless radio operators 90–1
Wollstonecraft, Mary 86
Women's Auxiliary Air Force 90
Women's Co-operative Movement 86
Women's Freedom League 84
Women's Liberal Association 86
Women's Police Service 142
Women's Police Volunteers 139–43
women's rights 27, 40, 83, 86–8
    in the workplace 83, 86–8
Women's Social and Political Union 43, 84
Women's Suffrage Journal, The 149
Women's Temperance movement 120, 121–2
Wood, Sir Henry 150
Woodford 131–2
Woods, John Adams 106–9
Woolf, Virginia 1, 43
Wordsworth, William 102
working classes 2, 23
Wortley Montagu, Edward 155
Wortley Montagu, Sir Edward 155–6
Wortley Montagu, Mary 155
Wortley Montagu, Lady Mary 134, 155–6
    Embassy Letters 155, 156
Wright, Joseph 30–1
Wright, Patience Lovell 28, 30–4

X-ray diffraction 158
X-ray microscopy 159

Yeats, W. B. 93
Yoruba tribe 80

Zog, King 76
zoology 72, 144